THE PERSISTENCE OF THE IDEOLOGICAL LIE:
THE TOTALITARIAN IMPULSE THEN AND NOW

THE PERSISTENCE OF THE IDEOLOGICAL LIE: THE TOTALITARIAN IMPULSE THEN AND NOW

DANIEL J. MAHONEY

BOOKS

NEW YORK • LONDON

2025

First American edition published in 2025 by Encounter Books,
an activity of Encounter for Culture and Education, Inc.,
a nonprofit, tax-exempt corporation.
Encounter Books website address: www.encounterbooks.com

Manufactured in the United States and printed on acid-free paper.
The paper used in this publication meets the minimum requirements
of ANSI/NISO Z39.48–1992 (R 1997)
(Permanence of Paper).

FIRST AMERICAN EDITION

LIBRARY OF CONGRESS CATALOGING-IN-PUBLICATION DATA

Information for this title can be found at the
Library of Congress website under the following
ISBN 978-1-64177-373-7 and LCCN 2024053685.

TABLE OF CONTENTS

*I've counted them all up: the teacher who laughs with
children at their God and at their cradle, is already ours.
The lawyer who defends an educated murderer by saying
that he's more developed than his victims and couldn't help killing
to get money, is already ours. Schoolboys who kill a peasant
just to see how it feels, are ours. Jurors who acquit criminals
right and left, are ours. The prosecutor who trembles in court
for fear of being insufficiently liberal is ours, ours.
Administrators, writers—oh, a lot of them, an awful lot of
them are ours, and they don't know it themselves!*

— DOSTOEVSKY, *Demons*

*The self-deification of mankind, to which Marxism gave
philosophical expression, has ended in the same way as all such
attempts, whether individual or collective: it has revealed
itself as the farcical aspect of human bondage.*

— LESZEK KOŁAKOWSKI, *Main Currents of Marxism*

*If only it were all so simple! If only there were evil people somewhere
insidiously committing evil deeds, and it were necessary only to
separate them from the rest of us and destroy them. But the line
dividing good and evil cuts through the heart of every human being.
And who is willing to destroy a piece of his own heart?*

— ALEKSANDR SOLZHENITSYN, *The Gulag Archipelago*

Our present system is unique in world history, because over and above its physical and economic constraints, it demands of us total surrender of our souls, continuous and active participation in the general, conscious lie. To this putrefaction of the soul, this spiritual enslavement, human beings who wish to be human cannot consent. When Caesar, having exacted what is Caesar's, demands still more insistently that we render unto him what is God's —that is a sacrifice we dare not make!

—ALEKSANDR SOLZHENITSYN, *From Under the Rubble*

Identity politics is not satisfied with the Christian account that there will always be an imbalance of payments that only God can redress through His infinite mercy. Identity politics demands a complete accounting, so that the score can be settled once and for all—or, if it cannot be settled, then held over the head of transgressors like a guillotine, in perpetuity.... The complete accounting that is needed requires ongoing investigations that clarify just how stained the transgressors are, and how pure the innocents are. This now seems to be the singular task of our colleges and universities, which have thoroughly renounced their ancient charge, dating from the founding of Plato's Academy in 387 B.C., of assisting students in ascending from mere opinion to knowledge and wisdom.

— JOSHUA MITCHELL, *American Awakening: Identity Politics and Other Afflictions of Our Time*

INTRODUCTION:
FROM IDEOLOGICAL NEGATION TO
THE AFFIRMATION OF THE REAL

THIS BOOK AIMS to provide nothing less than a full-throated defense of moral and political sanity against the latest eruptions of ideological mendacity in our time. Its thesis is simple enough, but it needs the full resources of applied political philosophy to explain with adequate clarity and depth. The thesis? That the "ideological" project to replace the only human condition we know with a utopian "Second Reality" oblivious to—indeed at war with—the deepest wellsprings of human nature and God's creation has taken on renewed virulence in the late modern world, just thirty-five years after the glorious anti-totalitarian revolutions of 1989.

This was not supposed to happen. Midcentury "progressive democracy," as the Hungarian moral and political philosopher Aurel Kolnai called it in 1950, had already revealed itself to be an "incomplete totalitarianism" that, nonetheless, was capable, he argued, of rivaling Communism and Nazism by morphing into a "Third Rider of the Apocalypse."[1] For a long time, Kolnai's forebodings about a totalitarian turn in democracy seemed exaggerated and not a little overwrought to me. But how prescient this analyst of the utopian mind turned out to be. That Third Rider has indeed come to threaten and repress, as Kolnai feared, all *essential opposition* to Autonomous Man, the human being defined by his desire to emancipate himself from the "alien powers" (as Marx called them) that subjugate Man. Included in these powers are all natural, transcendent, and inherited limits to human will. The totalitarian impulse has thus survived the "official" collapse of the classic totalitarian regimes and ideologies of the twentieth century and has come out strengthened, and less "incomplete," in decisive respects. For a long time, Kolnai wrote, democracy, no matter how "progressive" its ultimate aspirations, had

[1]

"contained and sheltered" precious "traditions of civilization and frag-
ments of liberty" that it now jettisons with irresponsible abandon. Its
"theory"—increasingly abstract, insatiable, unremitting—has come to triumph over its once salutary "practice." The endless self-radicalization of
democracy predicted by Alexis de Tocqueville nearly two hundred years
ago has come to pass with unerring and unnerving accuracy.

As a result, the constraints and limits that informed the democracies of
old have largely been replaced by contempt for the enduring verities that
once guided the exercise of human freedom. As Leo Strauss wrote around
the same time in his illuminating 1953 essay "Progress or Return," the
crucial error, the root of the evil, was the replacement of the once-venera-
ble distinction between "good and evil" with the ever-shifting "distinction"
between "progress and reaction."[2] That ever-moving distinction not only
distorted our understanding of the human world but could be readily in-
voked to justify draconian efforts to restrict civilized liberty, ordered liberty, in the name of the "Progress" of humanity and the "democratic idea."
It is no accident (as the Marxists like to say) that Marxist-Leninists in
the Soviet Union and elsewhere prided themselves on their commitment
to "Progressive Doctrine," in their view the only genuine meaning of democracy rightly understood. The woke closer to home are self-described
"progressives" as well, quick to label those who disagree with them as "re-
actionaries," "racists," and "oppressors," who must be silenced, shamed,
and "canceled" in order to promote a fictive liberation and justice, to bury
"racism," "colonialism," "sexism," and "transphobia" once and for all. In
today's salient cultural and political dispensation, university administrators, activists, and DEI (Diversity, Equity, and Inclusion) officers crudely
replace liberal education and Socratic interrogation with cliché-ridden
orthodoxy indistinguishable from indoctrination. To be sure, America
remains a largely if only partially free country, though markedly less so
than even in the recent past. But the totalitarian impulse lies at the heart
of this ascendant ideology of cultural negation and civilizational repudiation, and several segments of civil society, along with progressives in
government, are committed to "saving democracy" by suffocating it. We

no longer live in a recognizably liberal age as a new authoritarian order imposes itself in the name of an obligatory "anti-authoritarianism." These troubling paradoxes go unnoticed, alas, by too many friends of liberty and human dignity.

If the American Framers were cautiously hopeful about the capacity of a republican people to govern themselves by "reflection and choice" (in the language of *Federalist* No. 1), they never confused human beings with angels who could solve the political problem once and for all. Their anthropology, their account of human nature and human motives, was sober, realistic, and devoid of both excessive optimism and debilitating pessimism. Their institutional arrangements drew on Locke and especially Montesquieu and those two thinkers' new science of power checking power in a modern republic at once representative and commercial. But the language and categories of virtue and vice, of good and evil, of sin and imperfection, still spoke powerfully to their hearts and minds. In them coexisted an admirable moderation formed from classical and Christian sources with a confidence in a sober and constrained version of modern progress. They never for a moment succumbed to what Eric Voegelin has so suggestively called "modernity without restraint," to utopian dreams and delusions. The political scientist Martin Diamond rightly called the American Revolution that rare sight to behold: "a revolution of sober expectations."

Like much of my previous writing and scholarship, this book is dedicated to defending decent, moderate, nonutopian, and nonideological politics by exposing the Ideological Lie for what it is. This effort has several components, some critical, some positive. Let me briefly enumerate them with the help of eminent guides: First, modern totalitarianism is revealed as the effectual truth of "modernity without restraint" (Eric Voegelin), the self-enslavement of human beings (Aurel Kolnai) that inexorably flows from jettisoning a sober and serious appreciation of the drama of good and evil within every human soul. As the Russian writer Aleksandr Solzhenitsyn argues in *The Gulag Archipelago*, the greatest anti-totalitarian work ever written, evil is never simply "localized" in

[3]

certain "oppressive" groups who are said to be its sole carriers and utterly beyond redemption. In truth, "The line dividing good and evil runs through the heart of every human being." Totalitarian ideologues lack self-knowledge because they refuse to turn the sword inward and fail to recognize their own capacity for what Solzhenitsyn calls "exuberant evil."[3]

Second, as the unjustly forgotten political theorist Gerhart Niemeyer argues in his wonderfully insightful 1971 book, *Between Nothingness and Paradise*,[4] it is the height of unreflective hubris to turn revolution into a "vocation" and to denounce the whole of creation as "sheer inhumanity" and a "gigantic deception." That insidious path—followed by François-Noël Babeuf and his "conspiracy of equals," by the Russian revolutionary movement of the nineteenth century, by Marxism in its Leninist, Stalinist, and Maoist forms, and by New Left and Third Worldist intellectuals everywhere—combines nihilism with a debased taste for violence and moral transgression.

Original sin, that moral taint that cannot be eliminated in this fallen sublunar world, does not mean, as Niemeyer puts it, that "*all* laws are unjust, *all* consciousness is false, *all* relations must be corrupt, *all* institutions appear oppressive." To say "No" to everything is to succumb to rank ingratitude and nihilistic despair. As Niemeyer perceptively argues, the "total critique of society" at the center of all ideological movements only leads to murderous and coercive politics and to a massive assault on political reason rightly understood. True prophets, the biblical ones, especially such as Isaiah and Amos, attack gross injustice and religious infidelity, while false prophets aim "to destroy the common acceptance of a divine creation and a created human nature." Political, philosophical, and religious wisdom in the West, before the ideological age, conceived healthy political life "as the order of *acting* within a cosmos of natures, rather than as a project of making both man and the world."[5]

Third, with the wise English conservative philosopher Roger Scruton, this book sees the "deconstruction" and "repudiation" of our Western inheritance not as an "'empowering' of the oppressed" but as a dangerous and destructive enterprise that madly invites us to "un-create and re-create the world" ad infinitum.[6] To reduce everything to rapacious "power" is to distort reality beyond recognition, and to drive love and friendship, benign authority, and civic comity from the human world. It is to trample on the Sacred and thus to do the Devil's work. It is Goethe's Mephistopheles who is committed to forever negating the *givenness* of the world, the world as it has been bequeathed to us.

These "heresies," as Roger Scruton called them, are essential elements or building blocks of the fictive "surreality" or Second Reality that the Ideological Lie presupposes and aims to put in place of the natural order of things. These widely held sophistries and distortions provide the animating core of the totalitarian impulse that is so alluring to intellectuals who have dedicated themselves to the hate-filled "total critique of society." If they are not all on the revolutionary barricades, they have deliberately and self-consciously corrupted what remains of the humanities and humanistic education. And they indulge tyranny and terror (think Mao's China, Castro's Cuba, or, more recently, Hamas) as morally superior to what remains of prosaic bourgeois democracy.

A quarter of a century ago, America still stood as a living reproach to the propensity of European elites (and the European Union) to think that a viable community could be built on the perilous foundations of negation and repudiation. America was still a proud and patriotic nation-state, a free people who largely rejected the intellectual party's preference for cynicism and nihilism. Americans, at least ordinary Americans, had not yet succumbed to the "lust for transgression which characterizes the philosophies of liberalism and liberation." The "silent majority" of Americans, still rooted in common sense and patriotic attachments, understood that no one had a "God-given right to destroy." Scruton saw that in recklessly tearing apart the "political *Lebenswelt*," the humanizing narratives of a shared political destiny made possible by admiration for the likes of the Framers and Abraham Lincoln, one never arrived at the "really real."[7] Instead, citizens are left disoriented, and especially the young, with a "moral void" accompanied by "cultural alienation" of the most debilitating kind. Repudiation and transgression

[5]

leave the soul cold and legitimate hopes dashed. In place of shared civic heroes and historical memories, ingratitude becomes the order of the day. Everyone becomes a "victim," and no one is truly a citizen in a community of memory. In the process, the world is desacralized, shorn of transcendence. In this crucial respect, American exceptionalism is no more. Even the French, at least the more sober among them, now think of political correctness as a dreaded American import. They have conveniently, if understandably, forgotten the European roots of the culture of repudiation in *la pensée de soixante-huit,* as the French called it—the thought of 1968, which combined moral antinomianism with admiration for left-wing totalitarianism.

One caveat is in order: by ideology I do not mean just any worldview or intellectual or political perspective that competes for the loyalty of acting men and women. Such perspectivism is both crude and lazy. It assumes that all moral and political judgments are mere assertions that cannot be adjudicated before the tribunal of reason. That is just another form of complacent nihilism. In contrast, this book aims to be an exercise in practical reason and applied political philosophy and not an "ideological" response to equally ungrounded ideological assertions. It follows the best critics of the totalitarian Lie, especially those from behind the Iron Curtain, who saw in ideology a mendacious assault on decent politics and the human soul. To oppose the ideological deformation of reality is at the same time to affirm the goodness of the created order.

This book thus aims not only to repudiate repudiation and the widespread nihilism of our time, but to affirm those enduring verities always worth affirming. With my friend and teacher Pierre Manent, I believe that the defense of decency and moderation is inseparable from a thoughtful reaffirmation of "liberty under the Law," not only the civic or constitutional law, but what the great thinkers of the West have called the Law of God, the Law of Nature, or the Law of Reason. As Manent rightly stresses, this is a "law that human beings did not make, as in the commandment 'thou shall not kill.'" Human life without authoritative

Law is both unlivable and finally unthinkable. Let me quote Manent's discerning words:

> *It is the law that grounds human dignity. If human beings cannot do as they wish with others or with themselves, this is because there is a Law that forbids it—a Law that is expressed in the Ten Commandments. The progressive injunction commands us, in the name of humanity, to leave behind what constitutes our humanity. In doing so we fail to realize that, by abandoning or weakening the fundamental Law, our much-vaunted "pragmatism" is left without a guiding principle.*[8]

In this light, the book you are about to read is thus as much an affirmation of the natural order of things, what an older wisdom called the Law of Reason, as a critique of the still remarkably persistent Ideological Lie. Logically, morally, spiritually, and politically, the critique and affirmation go hand in hand. Such is the conviction that has guided my work over the last thirty-five years, whether writing on noble statesmanship, totalitarianism, the "conservative foundations of the liberal order," the "humanitarian" subversion of the Christian religion, the antinomianism that informs the thought of 1968, or the profound anti-totalitarian moral witness of Aleksandr Solzhenitsyn, or the wise and discerning thought of Raymond Aron, Pierre Manent, and Roger Scruton.

This book also provides an analysis of the "corruption," as Montesquieu put it, of a political order, the regime of modern liberty, to which I remain deeply committed. We in the Western democratic world have increasingly succumbed to what Montesquieu in *The Spirit of the Laws* called the "spirit of extreme equality" where "regulated democracy" gives way to a false and untenable equality that can only lead to "servitude" (see Book 8, chapter 3). Democracy, too, needs to affirm limits, constraints, hierarchies, and legitimate authority, if it is not to give way to moral anarchy, endless civic strife, and, in the end, a barely concealed form of despotism. As the sociologist Dominique Schnapper (the daughter of

[7]

Raymond Aron), another French friend of mine, wrote in her book *The Democratic Spirit of Law*:

> To maintain democratic order, we must resist the temptation of condemning indiscriminately all concrete achievements, from the best to the most controversial or the most reprehensible, in the name of an absolute and theoretical conception of what democracy should be.... It is utopian to want to rebuild the world from scratch every morning.[9]

With those wise and trenchant words, I invite the reader to turn to the body of the text, where I take aim at the latest instantiations of the Ideological Lie masquerading as another form of emancipation.

ACKNOWLEDGEMENTS

A BOOK, AT LEAST one that aims to be thoughtful and serious, cannot be written without the support of a community of friends and interlocutors who give life (and the intellectual life) its moments of joy, delight, and a shared and invigorating sense of purpose. Among them I happily acknowledge Paul Seaton, Ralph C. Hancock, Pierre Manent, Giulio de Ligio, Philippe Bénéton, Jack Fowler, Ignat Solzhenitsyn, Dan & Lori Kelly, Geoffrey Vaughan, Marc Guerra, Trevor Shelley, Steve Gardner, Jacob Howland, Tony Traylor, and David DesRosiers, among others.

Many of the chapters in this book began as pieces in *Law and Liberty*, *The American Mind*, and the *Claremont Review of Books* and have since been revised, expanded, and further developed. Others are new to the book. All were written with this book in mind and thus as self-consciously part of a larger and more sustained critique of the Ideological Lie. I happily thank such consummate earlier editors as Brian Smith, John Grove, Lee Trepanier, Seth Barron, Spencer Klavan, Mike Sabo, John Kienker, and Charles Kesler, as well as the generous support of Tom Klingenstein and Ryan Williams at the Claremont Institute.

A final word of deep-seated appreciation to Roger Kimball for his continuing confidence in my work and to the support of all the good folks at Encounter Books, including Sam Schneider, Lauren Miklos, Elizabeth Bachman, and my truly gifted copy editor, Luke Lyman. Their competence, expertise, and friendliness are deeply appreciated now as in the past.

DANIEL J. MAHONEY
June 7, 2024

CHAPTER 1

THE PATH TOWARD WOKE DESPOTISM AND BEYOND

As the disciples of the New Left gained purchase over the great bureaucracies, they advanced the revolution through a process of relentless negation: it gnawed, chewed, smashed, and disintegrated the entire system of values that came before it. And their strategy was ingenious: the capture of America's institutions was so gradual and bureaucratic, it largely escaped the notice of the American public, until it burst into consciousness following the death of George Floyd.

— CHRISTOPHER F. RUFO,
America's Cultural Revolution: How the Radical Left Conquered Everything

A SPECTER—TO BORROW a phrase from Karl Marx—is haunting the United States and the Western world more broadly: the specter of woke despotism. Most disturbingly, its epicenter is in the United States, a land once gloriously immune from the ideological and totalitarian temptations that so haunted and deformed European politics in the twentieth century. As Christopher Rufo demonstrates in his indispensable book *America's Cultural Revolution*, the woke revolution has been gaining traction for a very long time and is now on the cusp of "controlling everything"[1] from our universities and corporations to the prestige media to the increasingly censorious network of "social media" that stands in for civic discourse in the United States today.

The summer of 2020 brought the nihilistic face of this cultural revolution into the open by means of its frontal assault on the symbols of the Old America. Statues of the great and good (among them Lincoln, Frederick Douglass, Saint Junípero Serra, Teddy Roosevelt, and Quaker abolitionists) were toppled or defaced, as were those of men deemed hopelessly evil—foremost among them the Confederate generals who, while fighting for an unjust cause, often displayed impressive courage and personal integrity (and some of whom, such as Robert E. Lee, believed slavery to be immoral). Cities burned as radicals, much of the political class, and almost all of the Democratic Party demanded the "defunding" of the police, an idea at once preposterous and profoundly immoral because of the harm it wreaks on the weak and vulnerable. The United States was denounced as "systematically racist," as fundamentally unjust and indeed genocidal, and thus beyond political repair. Civic courage to confront this scandalous falsehood was in woefully short supply as intellectuals, journalists, and politicians competed to mouth revolutionary slogans worthy of the Jacobins and Bolsheviks, excusing violence and mayhem on a mass scale. Too many who knew better remained silent. Authentic liberals, as opposed to the conventionally radical, were a vanishing breed.

As a result, what I have called a "culture of hate"[2] replaced what remained of the old civilities, and national self-loathing became morally obligatory. As Rufo powerfully illustrates, educated suburban women, corporate executives, and our colleges and universities (with only a few exceptions) succumbed to the "Great Refusal" originally heralded by such thinkers as Herbert Marcuse, Angela Davis, and the revolutionary New Left in the 1960s (*ACR*, 1–88). The existing order, they had insisted, must be rejected root and branch in the name of "democratic Communism," an oxymoron if there ever was one. In the summer of 2020, tedious ideological clichés long ascendant on college campuses, such as the aforementioned "systematic racism," "white supremacy," "male supremacy," "neocolonialism," "genocidal capitalism," and "heterosexism," became current in the mainstream. The Great Refusal was underway in high gear.

Black Lives Matter (BLM), an insidious organization founded by militant, self-proclaimed "trained Marxists," admirers of Mao and Che who denounced the market economy, the bourgeois family, and biblical religion in the shrillest terms, was celebrated by craven, self-hating elites. Ideological fanatics (and grifters) were massively funded by a corporate establishment trying to buy protection, one whose own political and cultural inclinations had already been warped by its managerial class's exposure to woke ideology during its college years. In a word, America's collective nervous breakdown during the summer of 2020 was preceded by a sixty-year "war of position," theorized by the Italian Marxist Antonio Gramsci and famously described by the German student activist Rudi Dutschke as a "long march through the institutions" (*ACR*, 36–52).

Douglass or Bell?

This "long march" of civic and intellectual subversion is richly and amply documented in Rufo's book. We see how revolutionary agitprop took pedagogic form in the influential writings of the Brazilian activist Paulo Freire, whose work paved the way for coercive "consciousness raising" in our schools and a frontal ideological assault on "Eurocentrist," "white supremacist," "heteropatriarchal," and "homophobic" modes of thinking and discourse (*ACR*, 145–58). The White Man, and Western civilization more broadly, became the Enemies par excellence. The bleak and angry nihilism of Derrick Bell and his students from Harvard Law School (who fanned out to teach at our leading universities and law schools) denied "people of color" any meaningful agency in a "system" that was monolithically repressive and racist to its core. These racially obsessed activist-scholars willfully denied the significant progress in race relations and racial justice in the United States that was there for all to see (*ACR*, 237–41). In doing so, they helped poison civic and intellectual life, sowing hatred and suspicion instead of mutual respect and mutual accountability.

Blacks who appealed to America's "color-blind" principles of liberty and equality and who affirmed our common humanity under "Nature and Nature's God," were derided by Bell and his disciples as "minstrels" (*ACR*, 237–31) and racists in disguise. Closer to our day, Nikole Hannah-Jones's 1619 Project (which we will examine at length later in the book) portrayed the United States as little better than Nazi Germany, substituting our slave plantations for Hitler's death camps and crematoria. Lincoln was derided as an incorrigible racist who did little or nothing to free the slaves (much of the new historiography risibly claims that they liberated themselves with no help from the Union Army). This toxic mixture

[13]

of race hatred, historical revisionism, and deep and abiding pessimism and despair offers no hope of a constructive future for black Americans. Critical Race Theory (CRT)—and sundry other radical doctrines—systematically deprives them of dignity and agency, both moral and civic. They are thus encouraged to bask in resentment and despair or to war with an evil "system."

Contrast these corrosive attitudes with those of Frederick Douglass, the great black abolitionist, orator, writer, and diplomat of the nineteenth century who fought first slavery and then race prejudice and discrimination, with rare determination and eloquence. He was a virile man who had no time of day for those who saw black men as helpless "victims." Though he often disagreed with Lincoln, he admired him, and he praised the U.S. Constitution in 1852 as a "Glorious Liberty Document."[3] He encouraged black Americans, including ex-slaves, to cultivate a spirit of resilience, pride, and self-reliance. He admired above all boldness, personal integrity, and independence of spirit. He was a critical but proud citizen of an American republic, whose principles he admired and whose sometimes-sordid practices he worked to redeem.

What better heroes do Americans have than Lincoln and Douglass—two noble human beings, one white, one black, who stood up to chattel slavery and in doing so vindicated the honor of the American republic? Their friendship, rooted in profound mutual admiration and respect, is a testament to the promise of America. Both would agree that virility, not passivity, and self-critical patriotism, not nihilistic self-loathing, is the spirit of the free man and the free American—especially when mixed with a dose of humility before the Most High. In contrast, hatred and resentment enervate souls and tear apart the bonds of civic friendship that unite free men and women. Without gratitude for the likes of Abraham Lincoln and Frederick Douglass, our republic is cast off from its moorings. Lincoln and Douglass remain civic and moral lodestars for a now-multiracial republic dedicated, nobly if imperfectly, to the proposition that "all men are created equal."

Winning the Language Game

Woke despotism has not yet won the day. There is still time for resistance, reversal, and reclamation. The woke spirit may have infiltrated the commanding heights of American society, as Rufo and others have established. That indeed poses a most daunting task. But among our resources is the very fact that nothing constructive or enduring can be sustained by the seething resentment, anger, and repudiation that it so recklessly promotes and relies on.

Let me now offer some initial advice for salvaging and renewing the spirit of American republicanism. In general, it is predicated on the thought articulated so well by George Orwell concerning the necessary hygiene of language. Ideology always seeks to commandeer and command language, to twist meaning for its own perfidious purposes. The ideological deformation of reality must be both resisted and exposed for the sake of the preservation of liberty and equality rightly understood.

Therefore, those who love our principles of justice—equality of rights, equality under the law, merit, and responsibility—must not be taken in by the alluring homonyms that give old and precious words radically new and pernicious meanings. As John O'Sullivan has written, those homonyms subvert "liberal democracy as it was understood by, say, Winston Churchill or FDR or John F. Kennedy or Ronald Reagan."[4] This counterfeit version of liberal democracy "is not really open to institutions and policies that run counter to its 'liberationist' instincts." It thus grows ever more hostile to fundamental freedoms in the name of "social justice," "equity," and a conception of "democracy" that runs roughshod over the self-government of a free people.

As endlessly evoked by woke ideologues, "social justice" has nothing to do with equal rights, equal opportunity, or the recognition of a common human dignity. "Social-justice warriors" are not interested in the careful weighing and balancing of the rival claims of the rich, poor, and everyone in between. Instead, they wish to tear down, to level, to "equalize" in a way that in the end necessitates the harshest tyranny.

Truth be told, that alluring and ubiquitous phrase from the summer of 2020—"black lives matter"—had nothing decent, humane, or universalist about it. In Orwellian fashion, the phrase meant to convey that only *some* black lives mattered—black lives that could be weaponized, but not those murdered in the summer of 2020 in Seattle's occupied Capitol Hill Autonomous Zone (CHAZ), for example, or in black neighborhoods in Chicago every weekend. Nor those of the victims who died as a direct result of defunding the police. A movement that forbids us on pain of cancellation from proclaiming the noble principle, inseparably biblical and American, that "All lives matter," is unworthy of fealty.

Likewise, the increasingly obligatory alphabetical agitprops must be resisted and challenged. These include DEI—the insidious initialism that justifies the new tyranny of coerced and bureaucratically imposed slogans, doctrines, and programs required by CRT. They include also our new and surreal LGBTQIA++ regime, unremitting in its obsession with "queerness," "transgenderism," and sexual "fluidity," notions unknown to Americans a half generation ago. Again, in classically Orwellian fashion, "diversity" as understood on college campuses and in corporate boardrooms demands absolute ideological uniformity. Blacks and women, and gays for that matter, who think independently or challenge the new "fissionism" (as the sociologist Peter Baehr calls it),[5] which denies any normative sexual differences rooted in biological nature between men and women, are relegated to the category of traitors to their race and gender.

Similarly, the once-noble word "equity" has been distorted beyond all recognition. No longer connoting fairness, balance, an effort to adjust a discrepancy, or an exception not covered by the letter of the law (as in Aristotle's *Ethics* or the Anglo-American common-law tradition), it now demands a perfect equality of outcomes for every race or ethnic group. As the journalist Barton Swaim put it in the pages of *The Wall Street Journal*, progressives who invoke this ideological reinvention of equity "believe … against all evidence, that any variance in success among individuals of different races must be the result of conscious or unconscious racism."[6] So understood, "equity" wars with human nature, and would require draconian tyranny if it were to be truly applied in practice. It has also led to patently unfair results—witness the quotas that minimize admissions for Jews and Asians in elite institutions such as Harvard and Yale. Nothing good can result from equity so construed except injustice, tyranny, and racial and social conflict, a new war of all against all.

"Inclusion" is equally dishonest and no less Orwellian: Those who believe in the color-blind constitution, who do not loathe their country, and who believe in the old verities and morality are not welcome in the woke university, law firm, corporation, or media outlet. The woke "community" is in truth as *exclusionary* as it gets. More broadly, DEI is a classic example of what the anti-totalitarian dissidents behind the Iron Curtain in the days before 1989 called the "Ideological Lie," a term popularized by Solzhenitsyn. Those who choose to live in its fictive "Second Reality," as Eric Voegelin so suggestively called it, quickly lose contact with the most elementary realities. In the end, they risk losing the capacity to distinguish truth from falsehood, good from evil, to see what even an open-eyed child can see. There is a better way, one in tune with the best resources of Western and American civic traditions.

No Compromise, No Surrender

This brings me to the final and most essential point. Every decent American must reject the quintessentially ideological move of locating evil exclusively in suspect groups who are said to be guilty for who they are and not what they have done. That is the heart of the matter and a core theme of this book. That was tried by the Jacobins, Bolsheviks, and Nazis with murderous consequences. Nor are some racial or "gender" categories composed exclusively of "innocent victims" bereft of sin and any capacity for wrongdoing. We are all capable of being "victims and executioners,"[7] as Albert Camus reminded us after the Second World War. In his great anti-totalitarian classic *The Gulag Archipelago*, Aleksandr Solzhenitsyn spoke liberating truth when he wrote that the "line between good and evil passes not through states, nor between classes, nor between political parties either—but right through every human heart—and through all human hearts."[8] That is the path of moral sanity and political decency recommended by both the unbelieving Camus and the Christian Solzhenitsyn. To believe otherwise is to falsify the human condition and to succumb to ideology and fanaticism.

Thus the Ideological Lie in its new woke instantiation must be rejected as the crucial first step toward overcoming the aspiring despotism of our woke tyrants. We do not yet face a full-scale totalitarian or ideological state, but the logic of totalitarianism has been institutionalized throughout government as well as civil society. The latter is truly something new: the classical liberal theorists of representative government could hardly have imagined a tyranny emanating from civil society rather than a self-aggrandizing state. The hour is indeed later than we would like to think. In this new situation, we must resist—courageously and self-consciously —a censorious cancel culture and the intoxication of increasingly brutal social-media mobs. We must resist but not emulate.

At the same time, we must not partake of or repeat racialist lies (whether by the dwindling band of old-fashioned racists or from the more pernicious and numerous new ideological ones) or repeat ideological lies we know to be false and destructive. We cannot become Václav Havel's "Greengrocerers"[9] who unthinkingly mimic such ideological clichés as "workers of the world unite" to which they have given little or no reflection. To be sure, we are not required to scream the truth in the city square on a regular basis. Prudence and even elemental common sense must dictate how we exercise our civic and moral integrity. But civic courage and no small dose of Churchillian fortitude are today prerequisite for moral and civic recovery, for winning our country back from the ideologues who so disdain it. There is no true moderation or civic equanimity without the courage to sustain it.

Rufo is right: our real choice is to be thoughtful, principled, and spirited "counterrevolutionaries" (*ACR*, 278–82). But we must not fight black racialism with an equally misguided white identity politics. Instead, we must take our stand with the principles of '76, the majestic courage of Lincoln and Frederick Douglass, the Christian gentlemanliness of Robert Woodson, who rightly insists that "1776 Unites," and the concern for stubborn facts that animates the great black social scientist Thomas Sowell, who rightly teaches that disparities are not coextensive with discrimination.[10]

As this litany indicates, our attachment to 1776 and everything it represents cannot be simpleminded or naïve—we must renew the wisdom of our forebears in light of the challenge of a thoroughgoing nihilism they could hardly have imagined. In this vein, we must recognize and acknowledge that we are more than a so-called propositional nation, even if we are a nation that should remain dedicated to noble self-evident truths. We are also a territorial democracy, with a history that is uniquely our own and with borders that demarcate us as a self-governing nation. As the political scientist Carson Holloway recently observed, in recent decades "Marriage has been redefined, public education has been used to indoctrinate the young in radical sexual ideologies, and religion has been marginalized—all while propositional-nation conservatives have been unaware that the nation's character has been marginalized."[11] That will not do. To be sure, America is unthinkable without abstract principles and what Alexis de Tocqueville called "general ideas" about liberty and equality.[12] But in order to sustain a regime of civilized liberty, we must kindle, safeguard, and renew the crucial moral and cultural preconditions of the free society.

One final note. In refusing to bow before woke ideology, especially the madness of gender ideology that wars against God's creation and the natural order of things, there is no better path to follow than to reaffirm the oldest and deepest truth, the bedrock truth of all political order and moral good sense: "So God created humankind in his image, in the image of God he created them; male and female he created them" (Genesis 1:27). This is a palpable truth rooted in both reason and revelation, as well as in the biological nature of human beings. It is inseparable from Natural Law. Gender ideology, in contrast, aims to create a fictive surreality at odds with the biological and social nature of human beings. Wishing 173 genders into existence doesn't make it so. And propagandizing the

[19]

young to this effect, and actively encouraging what is in effect physical and spiritual mutilation, is profoundly immoral and irresponsible.

A serious conversation, lively and respectful, must be inaugurated among all those who wish to preserve moral and political sanity in our country today, a true coalition of the brave. In doing so, we must remain at once spirited and moderate, conservative and counterrevolutionary, manly and humane. At the same time, we must not confuse high prudence and genuine moderation, always to be cherished, with the "false reptile prudence" that Edmund Burke warned against among false friends of liberty who refused to stand up to the "armed doctrine"[13] of Jacobinism in his own time. There is in truth no middle way between the Great Affirmation of Reality and the Great Refusal of Western civilization as we have known it. Our work is all the more difficult since this self-hating Refusal has now more or less become public orthodoxy. But the battle can and must be fought and won.

CHAPTER 2

THE NEW AGE OF UNIFORMITY

IN ADDITION TO all this, we live in a new age of enforced uniformity, prosecuted in the name of preserving "our democracy" and keeping "disinformation" and "Far Right lies" at bay. The Harvard intellectual historian James Hankins has aptly spoken of an "information oligarchy"[1] that is committed to maintaining and enforcing its monopoly on the truth. In this surreal world of "democratic" uniformity, certain "truths" are said to be beyond challenge or question. To challenge them with evidence, logic, and a more faithful regard for the truth is to risk being dismissed as an extremist or conspiracy theorist. The independent minded, those who refuse to bow before what George Orwell so memorably called "smelly little orthodoxies,"[2] are candidates to be canceled and confined to the category of those beyond the pale. The Left has a preferred name for this: those who resist the pressure of intellectual conformity, of stifling political correctness, are "enemies of democracy."

But the "democracy forever" narrative pushed and enforced by the information oligarchy is, truth be told, built on a foundation of lies, beginning with the mendacious Russia hoax—the claim that desultory Russian disinformation promoted on social media made the difference in the 2016 election, and the even bigger lie that Donald Trump colluded with the Russians before and after the 2016 election. Those lies are still promoted by leftist elites even though there is not a shred of evidence to support them. They tore the country apart for the four years of Donald Trump's presidency and made effective governance all but impossible. And yet the endless repetition of these lies—promoted aggressively by the political class, the mainstream media, and even by powerful elements within the FBI and the CIA—were, and still are, in elite circles, considered to be a sine qua non of one's commitment to democratic values.

More broadly, the regnant narrative prohibited a meaningful public debate about the origins of the COVID-19 virus, the efficacy and consequences of long-term COVID-19 lockdowns, the effectiveness of vaccines and boosters, and, yes, the fairness of the 2020 presidential election. With the release of the so-called Twitter Files by the independent journalist Matt Taibbi, we now know that genuinely independent-minded voices, some of impeccable background and expertise who aimed to clarify the truth about these matters, were silenced at the urging of the FBI, important elements of the Deep State, and dominant woke personnel within the social-media companies themselves.

The FBI knew perfectly well that Hunter Biden's laptop—potentially containing the most questionable and corrupt business dealings between the Biden family and the Chinese and Ukrainian governments and their business subordinates—was no product of Russian disinformation. But they egregiously lied to the social-media companies who then censored the *New York Post*'s perfectly accurate story from October 2020 in order to prevent damage to Biden's electoral prospects just a few weeks before the 2020 election. Fifty-one relatively high-placed former intelligence officials then claimed, without an iota of evidence, that the revelations about the Biden-family corruption had all the hallmarks of classic Russian disinformation. Most disturbing of all, unquestionably affirming these lies immediately became a requirement of maintaining one's commitment to our "imperiled democracy." That is how the woke regime solidifies control.

While Trump and his more fevered partisans made some outlandish and unsubstantiated claims about the 2020 election being stolen hook, line, and sinker, the elite media forbade any discussion of how rapidly changing election laws in every state in the Union facilitated the prospects for significant electoral corruption. With the deliberate manipulation of social media, and with government-approved and promoted "cancellations" and coordinated mendacity by the FBI and its minions, one can hardly speak of a truly free and fair election even if no voting machines were hacked. None of that justified the lawlessness displayed by some unarmed Trump supporters at the Capitol on January 6, 2021. But "election denialism" did not begin in November of 2020.

The January 6, 2021, riot was hardly the "insurrection" of legend. And it was hard not to notice that those same politicians and commentators who were quick to denounce incipient fascism and an antidemocratic "insurrection" that threatened "our democracy" had remained silent during an earlier insurrection: the organized mayhem and violence in American cities during the summer and fall of 2020 that took so many lives and destroyed so many businesses, all in the name of "racial justice." During this earlier assault on American democracy, "no enemies to the Left" was the guiding rule of everyone from *The New York Times* editorial board to Bill Kristol's *Bulwark*, where Trump Derangement Syndrome is still so alive and on display. Whatever happened to prudence and moderation and an even-handed commitment to truth and the rule of law? It was nowhere to be seen in the politically correct establishment.

The seasoned journalist Lance Morrow, an old-fashioned liberal and an admirable defender of civic good sense, noted in the last year of the Trump presidency that while Trump habitually boasted and exaggerated in the most obvious of ways, his cultured despisers adopted massive ontological lies with impunity. Is there an iota of evidence to support the claim that human beings are not embodied persons but rather can choose one (or more) of 173 gender identities (and counting)? Is America really the most racist country in the history of the world? Are disparities among individuals and groups always a sign of discrimination and injustice? On the more specifically factual front, do the police really hunt down and murder thousands of black men each year, as many Americans seem to believe? Is an unborn child merely a blob of jelly or a part of a woman's body in the manner of a kidney or liver as the pro-choice movement insists? A moment of reflection suggests that a precondition for being politically correct today is to parrot one untruth after another, while immediately and often cruelly castigating those who refuse to deny their rational judgment and moral good sense. Political correctness can justly be called systematic and coercive mendacity at work. Whatever it is, it is hardly "scientific" or self-evident.

The ideological Left's claim to a monopoly of truth is thus impossible to countenance. It is also a significant departure from an earlier leftism that was all about jettisoning the very idea of truth. Just a few years ago, former President Barack Obama, a moderate leftist, told us that democracy is incompatible with any affirmation of "absolute truth."[3] The famous, or once-famous, pragmatist philosopher Richard Rorty insisted that everything is "contingent" all the way down—there is in the end no truth and no knowable or ascertainable structure of reality. Indeed, he once expressed incredulity in the pages of the *New Republic* (July 1991) that the late Václav Havel could sincerely advocate "living in truth,"[4] because there is no such thing as normatively binding truth. The postmodern Left, once relativistic from top to bottom and disdainful of a normative human nature and a binding moral law, now claims to speak the Truth and nothing but the Truth on all political matters. Should we be credulous enough to fall for this self-evident lie? I hardly think so.

The Crisis of the West Reconsidered

Let us bring things up to date. From Sydney to London to untold numbers of American college campuses, we hear incendiary cries for destroying the Jewish state, for a new Jihad or global intifada, all in the name of a purportedly noble and just "anticolonialist" struggle. Tens of thousands march in major European cities and with frenzied glee defend the indefensible. "From the river to the sea," cry the mobs of Islamists, Palestinians, activists, and radicals, shamelessly announcing their own genocidal sympathies and intent.

The so-called crisis of the West is nothing new. In 1949, the political philosopher Leo Strauss lamented that the main currents of social science in the United States, and in the Western world more broadly, could not understand tyranny for what it was since they were blindly committed to the absurd position that "facts" had nothing to do with "values." He added that a social science that could not speak reasonably— and forcefully—about the evil that is tyranny (especially in its modern ideological forms) was no better than a medical science that could not name and describe cancer. In the following decade, Raymond Aron and Hannah Arendt brought the full arsenal of political philosophy to bear on the "novel" form of tyranny that was totalitarianism and, in the process, mourned the indulgence of so many intellectuals toward it.

In 1964, James Burnham published a still-potent and relevant book called *The Suicide of the West*, where he took aim at Western self-hatred, romanticism about what would soon be called the Third World (some of which came to resemble "Caliban's kingdoms,"[5] in the striking and provocative words of Paul Johnson), and the degeneration of a once-noble and hardy liberalism into rank sentimentality, free-floating compassion, and a suicidal preference for our murderous and tyrannical enemies over our sometimes-imperfect friends and even our own country and civilization.

By 1970, the great English writer and journalist Malcolm Muggeridge wrote with eloquence and biting wit about "The Great Liberal Death Wish" in a seminal 1970 essay by that same name in *Esquire*. Muggeridge saw in the decayed liberal mind a perverse preference for nihilistic self-flagellation that led to the systematic "depreciating and deprecating" of "every aspect of our Western way of life." God and all moral certitudes were dethroned even as a "Praetorian Guard of ribald students, maintained at the public expense," were "ready at the drop of a hat to go into action, not only against their own weak-kneed bemused academic authorities, but also against any institution or organ for the maintenance of law and order still capable of functioning, especially the police." These words could have been written in the summer of 2020 amidst the violence, mayhem, and ritualistic self-flagellation that followed the death of George Floyd, or in the hours and days after the savage Hamas assault on Israeli innocents on October 7, 2023. Muggeridge went on to opine that if and when the West falls, it will not be the result of a barbarian invasion nor the murderous enmity of Communists, fascists, and Nazis, but because of the suicidal death wish of a liberalism gone badly awry. It is hard to say that Muggeridge was wrong.

The better liberals, humane and decent people, are rightly shocked by professors, students, and activists who celebrate or apologize for the savage nihilism of Hamas or who think that these cruel ideologues and

[25]

terrorists, heedless to the lives of their own people, whose deaths they relish for the propaganda value, somehow represent the legitimate interests of the Palestinian people. But what reason do we have for being surprised? English departments everywhere have given up teaching literature and humane letters and now specialize in the hate-filled jargon that defines "postcolonial" studies and discourse (more on this to come). "Intersectionality" is the order of the day—everyone who desires to be ideologically correct must unthinkingly parrot demands for CRT, gender ideology, abortion on demand, environmental extremism, sympathy and support for radical regimes and ideologies, contempt for religion and traditional morality, and a hatred of the West—above all for Israel, which is freely and ludicrously compared to apartheid South Africa and, most obscenely of all, Nazi Germany. DEI departments on most campuses enforce this new regime in a totalitarian spirit that is hardly "soft" or benign. For too long, economistic and anti-intellectual conservatives thought this had little to do with the "real world" and still proudly sent their children to utterly corrupt but still-prestigious universities and liberal-arts colleges. But as the journalist Andrew Sullivan likes to say, "We are all living on college campus now."[6]

Political correctness has been omnipresent for many years now, but somehow former Utah Governor Jon Huntsman, the quintessentially "moderate" politician, just noticed: after witnessing the temerity of the University of Pennsylvania's response to its mob of anti-Semitic agitators, he decided he could no longer be a benefactor of the corrupt institution. He is a decent human being, and I am glad he is appalled by the fact that UPenn was incapable of truly, unequivocally condemning what Hamas so brutally did to innocents on October 7, 2023. But why precisely was he surprised? UPenn was only being itself when it shamelessly indulged the enemies of Israel—and Western civilization. This is a university that took down, as if in a parody of political correctness, a picture of William Shakespeare in its English department. It regularly encourages every manifestation of crude, ritualistic anti-Western and "anticolonial" ideology.

The institution has long hounded conservative and other inde-pendent-minded faculty (and students) for not toeing the party line. Progressive ideology requires absolute fealty to the cause. To be sure, many Arabs and Palestinians (and their Western sympathizers) casual-ly give way to Jew-hatred. But progressives hate Israel mainly because they hate themselves and the Western world of which they are a part, though that self-loathing has quickly given way to fierce and crude anti-Jewish rhetoric and behavior. A figure long at the head of this charge, the radical intellectual and celebrated linguist Noam Chomsky, once accused Cambodian refugees of exaggerating the "excesses" of Pol Pot and the Khmer Rouge and wrote a foreword to a book by the French Holocaust denier Robert Faurisson.[7] Chomsky had no real deep affinity for monstrous regimes, but he was adamantly committed, and remains committed, to the view that the United States, and the Western world more broadly, is the primary author of evil in the world. Chomsky em-bodies the reductio ad absurdum of self-flagellating radicalism. On the left, he is still perversely celebrated as a courageous truth teller.

Writing in *The Abolition of Man* in 1943, the Christian apologist and man of letters C. S. Lewis wondered why our contemporary "men without chests," who had abandoned both reason and faith, who confused moral judgment with mere emotivism, and who belittled the virile virtues and the essential connections between reason and a spirited regard for liberty and civilization, were surprised by the inevitably destructive consequences of their doctrines. In words that stick to memory and that are as relevant as ever, Lewis writes:

> *In a sort of ghastly simplicity, we remove the organ and demand the function. We make men without chests and expect of them virtue and enterprise. We laugh at honour and are shocked to find traitors in our midst. We castrate and bid the geldings be fruitful.*

Those false liberals who actively supported the progressivist degrada-tion of our colleges and universities ought to be ashamed of themselves.

Those who marched with the totalitarian Marxists and Maoists of BLM (and who now predictably cheer Hamas on) in the summer of 2020—including foolish white progressives such as Senator Mitt Romney—are complicit in the madness that has taken hold of our political culture. They are also fools, naïfs.

As the Russianist Gary Saul Morson argued in a powerful piece that appeared in *The Wall Street Journal* ("Dostoevsky Knew: It Can Happen Here," October 18, 2023), those ideologues and intellectuals who justify the unjustifiable would do it to us if they had the chance. As Morson argues, the militant "anticolonialism" that is regnant today on our campuses and in bien-pensant intellectual circles is only the latest totalitarian ideology to justify the destruction of their "designated enemies." And the soft leftists—the naïve fellow travelers—always go first. One thinks of the politically correct bourgeoisie in Saint Petersburg, as described so vividly in Solzhenitsyn's *The Red Wheel* (March 1917), who proudly wore red and waved red flags (for two hundred years the color of the radical Left) to display their fine feelings and progressive leanings. They were the first to be condemned as class enemies and marched off to the camps in Lenin's new totalitarian dispensation. It is high time for their American counterparts to be mugged by reality before it is too late for them—and for the rest of us.

Sources and Suggested Readings

ON THE MULTIPLE WAYS in which a massive change of the rules in the midst of the COVID-19 epidemic influenced the outcome of the 2020 election, see Mollie Hemingway, *Rigged: How the Media, Big Tech, and the Democrats Seized Our Elections* (Washington, DC: Regnery, 2021).

ON SOCIAL SCIENCE's inability to see twentieth-century tyranny for what it was and to describe it as it is, see the opening pages of Leo Strauss, *On Tyranny: Corrected and Expanded Edition, Including the Strauss–Kojève Correspondence* (Chicago: University of Chicago Press, 2013).

THE NEW AGE OF UNIFORMITY

JUDICIOUSLY CHOSEN EXCERPTS from the writings on totalitarianism by Hannah Arendt and Raymond Aron, among others, can be found in *The Great Lie: Classic and Recent Appraisals of Ideology and Totalitarianism* (Washington, DC: ISI Books, 2011).

JAMES BURNHAM'S 1964 recently reissued classic, *Suicide of the West: An Essay on the Meaning and Destiny of Liberalism* (New York: Encounter Books, 2014), brilliantly captures the self-destructive tendencies inherent in the psychology of decayed liberalism.

MALCOLM MUGGERIDGE'S prescient and deliciously biting 1970 *Esquire* essay, "The Great Liberal Death Wish," can be found in abridged form at various venues on the internet. The full text can be found in Ian A. Hunter, ed., *Things Past: Malcolm Muggeridge, An Anthology* (New York: William Morrow and Company, 1979), 220–38.

FOR EXAMPLES of Chomsky's limitless contempt for imperfect but free and decent societies, and his ample indulgence toward totalitarian ones of the Left and the Right, see Peter Collier, ed., *The Anti-Chomsky Reader,* (New York: Encounter Books, 2004).

C.S. LEWIS'S powerful and memorable words close the first of the three sections of his incomparable *The Abolition of Man*, originally published in 1943 and available today from Harper Collins (New York: 2015) among other publishers.

CHAPTER 3

THE PERSISTENCE OF THE LIE: DESPOTISM OLD AND NEW

A S THE GREAT anti-totalitarian Russian writer and Nobel laureate Aleksandr Solzhenitsyn noted time and again, violence and lies are the twin pillars, the soul-destroying foundations, of Communist regimes in every time and clime, from Moscow to Beijing to Havana. In the words of Martin Malia, the author of the magisterial *The Soviet Tragedy*, Communism has a recognizable nature, one incompatible in any time or place with liberty and human dignity. Solzhenitsyn knew of what he spoke. He had spent eleven years in prison, camps, and exile, where, thankfully, the scales of ideology fell from his eyes. He experienced the Ideological Lie from within. As a result, as we have already noted in our earlier discussion of *The Gulag Archipelago*, he became one of the most courageous and consequential moral witnesses of the twentieth century.

Through bitter experience, Solzhenitsyn arrived at this firm conclusion: The Communist regime and ideology are in decisive respects at odds with the deepest wellsprings of human nature and with the moral norms that constitute a free and decent society. How can one attain liberty worthy of human beings when private property is summarily abolished or dramatically curtailed, the traditional family is assaulted and its prerogatives radically circumscribed, religion is cruelly persecuted, and humane national loyalty and traditions are replaced by an abstract and coercive utopianism based on contempt for the cultural and civilizational inheritance? As Solzhenitsyn wrote in his 1973 "Letter to the Soviet Leaders," Marxist ideology was not "only decrepit and helplessly antiquated" by that year, but "even during its best decades it was totally mistaken in its predictions and was never a science."[1] The Soviet leaders were, of course, not prepared at that time to take in and act upon Solzhenitsyn's sage insights. Contrary to legend, Communism was never good "in theory" as so many are wont to say today (including almost all the students I have taught in recent years). The theory itself demands violence against human nature since Communism's four "abolitions," those of property, the family (bourgeois or otherwise), religion, and the nation, are profoundly at odds with the nature and needs of human beings and the very structure of social and political reality.

But the truly dramatic implosion of European Communism between 1989 and 1991 has not led to the so-called end of History (far from it) or even the cessation of ideological politics. New forms of ideological mendacity have risen in the place of the totalitarian Lie precisely *because that Lie has never been truly and widely understood or repudiated.* This chapter will trace the movement from ideological mendacity in its classic totalitarian form to the new forms of ideological despotism that today threaten Western liberty, the search for truth, and the integrity of human souls. As I will show, the two forms of the Lie are by no means unrelated.

Solzhenitsyn on the Ideological Lie

As Solzhenitsyn himself testified in one of the most profound and soul-shaking books of the twentieth century, the three-volume *Gulag Archipelago*, the great Ideological Lie "gives evildoing its long-sought justification and gives the evildoer the necessary steadfastness and justification" (GA, 77). "Macbeth's self-justifications were feeble—and his conscience devoured him," he famously observed (GA, 77). In their guilt and moral derangement, Macbeth and Lady Macbeth still bowed before the requirements of conscience and literally went mad as a result of their crimes.

But totalitarian ideology negates conscience and dismisses the moral law of which it is a dark reflection as an antiquated justification for class oppression, a tool of the forces of "privilege" and oppression (rhetoric that again has become all too familiar). In this grotesque transvaluation of values, whatever promotes world-transforming revolution is necessary and good, and whatever stands in its way is, by definition, retrograde and evil. The age-old distinction between good and evil, right and wrong, is replaced by the morally corrupting distinction between "progress" and "reaction." But the movement of History, ideologically defined, is hardly coextensive with moral progress. Moreover, what is right and wrong does not fundamentally change from epoch to epoch or from culture to culture. The old is not necessarily antiquated and the "new" need not entail a moral advance. Surely, the tragedies of the twentieth century ought to have taught us to question the ideology of inevitable "historical progress" and to reaffirm the need to respect the elementary distinction between right and wrong at the heart of all authentic moral and political judgment. Without that reaffirmation, civilization and the soul will lose their luster and surely will perish.

Progressive ideologies closer to home draw on the same mix of moral nihilism and rage at the limits inherent in human nature, our society, and even the very structure of reality. Their rage reveals a crude division of the world that localizes evil in a specific (and an utterly dispensable) group of class, race, or gender oppressors, as well as unrelieved contempt for old verities, traditions, and points of view. At Bard College, several years ago we saw three student activists, contemporary "Red Guards," *charged by their administration to "decolonize"* the college library of books deemed ideologically suspect. One could add thousands of other examples, each as depressing and alarming as the others. Such exercises in the groves of the academy are no longer exceptional or unexpected. Orwellian book banning in the name of "progress"! This is blatant authoritarianism dressed up as antiracism and moral preening. No progress there, only reprehensible moral and intellectual regression.

As Solzhenitsyn has indisputably established, the Ideological Lie deceives at a very fundamental level. Those who perceive themselves as "innocent victims," bereft of sin and any capacity for wrongdoing, or as agents of historical "progress," become puffed up with hubris and feel themselves to be infallible. They thus become oppressors with little or no sense of limits or moral restraint. In Albert Camus's memorable words that we have already quoted, we must instead aim to be "neither victims nor executioners." That is the path of civic self-respect and spiritual renewal.

[33]

The Great Imperative to "Live Not by Lies!"

On the day Solzhenitsyn was arrested in Moscow, February 12, 1974—
and the day before he was forcibly exiled to the West (first to West
Germany, then by choice to Switzerland, then to Vermont)—he issued
a truly dramatic proposal to his compatriots through the samizdat (the
USSR's underground self-publishing ring), which was printed as well in
a hurried translation in *The Washington Post*. That pungent and memorable text, "Live Not by Lies!," since expertly retranslated,[2] was a clarion
call for his fellow citizens to recover civic pride and self-respect even in
the absence of a regime of political and civil liberty. Solzhenitsyn argues
that nothing but bloodshed, tyranny, and tragedy could result from the
revolutionary illusions of "conceited youths who sought, through terror,
blood uprising, and civil war, to make the country just and content" (*TSR*,
557). Solzhenitsyn at once rejects the "vileness of means" that "begets"
the "vileness of the result" (and the other way around). "For violence
has nothing to cover itself with but lies, and lies can only persist through
violence" (*TSR*, 557). The twin pillars of ideological despotism—violence
and lies—must be rejected at their very source along with the utopian
illusions that inspire them. Drugged with ideology, and with the cruel impatience that marks those inspired by utopian illusions, an entire
people are led down the path of violence and lies off the cliff, like the
demoniac Gadarene swine so vividly described in the Gospel of Luke
(Luke 8:26–39). Another truly humane path forward must be found.

Solzhenitsyn finds the path to liberation through a self-conscious decision by sturdy, self-respecting souls not to participate in lies: "Personal
non-participation in lies!" (*TSR*, 558) as he strikingly puts it in the imperative (Václav Havel would reformulate this imperative as "living in
truth" in his well-known 1978 essay "The Power of the Powerless," an
essay where he favorably cites Solzhenitsyn no less than four times).
Already in the 1973 letter, Solzhenitsyn had proclaimed the "universal,
obligatory force-feeding with lies" to be the "most agonizing aspect of
existence" in the Soviet Union, "worse than all our material miseries,

worse than any lack of civil liberties" (*EW*, 127). Of course, he noted, no one is morally obliged to scream the truth at the top of his lungs in the public square (*TSR*, 558). But persons of integrity must not knowingly reinforce the web of totalitarian mendacity. Men and women of good will must not denounce coworkers or neighbors who are charged with self-evident lies by a lawless state just as we must resist a cruelly censorious cancel culture and the intoxication of brutal Twitter (now "X") mobs. This path of nonparticipation in lies will entail sacrifices, perhaps the loss of jobs or the barring of children from promising careers, but not the inevitable internment in prison or camp characteristic of the Stalin (and even Lenin) years in the Soviet Union. When Solzhenitsyn wrote his searing manifesto in early 1974, the edifice of ideological mendacity was already "flaking" as he put it, and would soon be exposed for the whole world to see. The situation demanded a judicious combination of personal steadfastness, spiritual integrity, and civic courage (*TSR*, 558).

Courage is required, but not necessarily martyrdom (Solzhenitsyn recognized that most human beings are not naturally courageous and that dissent in post-Stalinist forms of Soviet-style Communism entailed fewer risks than in the Lenin and Stalin years of classic totalitarianism). If the camp of those who refused to live by lies were multiplied to include thousands, even tens of thousands, then Solzhenitsyn and other Russians "will not recognize our country!" But if Solzhenitsyn's compatriots instead choose the path of passivity, acquiescence, and the habitual assent to grotesque lies, then they would indeed reveal themselves to be "worthless, hopeless," and deserving of "scorn." Quoting Russia's national poet, Pushkin, Solzhenitsyn devastatingly adds:

> *Why offer herds their liberation?*
> . . . .
> *Their heritage each generation*
> *The yoke with jingles, and the whip.* (*TSR*, 560)

Speaking to Us in A New Situation

What, one might ask, does Solzhenitsyn's noble appeal to spiritual integrity and civic pride have to say to us in the United States, an ostensibly free country faced by the growing specter of woke despotism? To be sure, ours is a new and different situation, even if parallels can be readily drawn. We do not live under the yoke of totalitarianism. Yet, a generation ago, a political scientist such as myself could readily and rightly declare that the United States was a country largely free of extremist ideological politics and parties and with no intelligentsia to speak of. A radicalized intelligentsia was instead typical of such countries as France and Russia, where a large part of the intellectual class assented to the moral nihilism and revolutionary politics represented by 1793 and 1917, respectively. American exceptionalism of the kind just described is, alas, no more. Our intelligentsia (including radical academics, professional activists, journalists who repudiate old norms of fairness and objectivity, myriad woke-minded persons in the high-tech sector, the whole industry dedicated to "diversity, equity, and inclusion," and advocates of socialism and even Communism in "progressive" circles) more and more resembles the intellectual class in Russia between 1860 and 1917, one dedicated at the same time to nihilism, ideological fanaticism, and contempt for patriotism and customary morality. In both cases, a culture of repudiation, as the late Roger Scruton calls it,[3] replaces moderation, common sense, and gratitude for our received inheritance. Even the savage nihilism and Jew-hatred of Hamas is shamelessly applauded in certain elite circles and on an alarming number of college campuses. The corruption runs deep, and nihilistic self-loathing has become de rigueur among the new purveyors of the Lie. We are confronted by a new form of what Jacob Talmon called "totalitarian democracy" in his classic work *The Origins of Totalitarian Democracy.*

Having grievously failed to come to terms with the Lie at the foundation of Communist totalitarianism, to pass on its lessons to the next generations, we are now reliving the ideological madness that gave rise

[36]

to unrelieved human tragedy in the first place. We risk restoring a world of victims and executioners, the very world Solzhenitsyn and Camus so powerfully warned against. Weren't the kulaks (the allegedly prosperous peasants) in the Soviet Union and the Jews in the Nazi orbit persecuted, harassed, and killed (and in the Nazi case industrially exterminated) far more for who they were than for anything anyone of them had done? Wasn't the bourgeoisie targeted for being "privileged" as if industriousness and success were always or usually a product of villainy and exploitation, an illusion or lie if there ever was one? Is the obsession with race, class, and gender in every level of education, in almost all cultural institutions, in journalism, in corporate America, and sports different in principle from the old totalitarian and ideological obsession with race and class enemies? If disparities and inequalities are identified always and everywhere with injustice and exploitation, we have an invitation to cruel, leveling, and fanatical despotism—to totalizing tyranny in the name of perfect equality. A page torn right out of Dostoevsky's *Demons*, as we shall see.

As importantly, how can the dignity of every person under God's creation thrive or even survive if we continue to think and act in such a grossly divisive manner? One is led to ask: Have we learned *nothing* from the political tragedies of the twentieth century? Where is the sobriety, the moral realism, that alone can give rise to mutual respect, free and decent politics, and realistic and durable change within a framework of critical respect for our country's, and our civilization's, admirable achievements? The fevered politics of purity and perfection are in every respect an enemy of the good, of mutual respect, and of shared liberty under the rule of law. If we don't recognize this elementary truth, and soon, we shall surely lose our civilizational soul and perhaps our freedoms, too.

Reasons for Hope

But there remain reasons for hope. An independent-minded liberal such as Bari Weiss, driven out of *The New York Times* at the beginning of the woke ascendancy in the summer of 2020, has self-consciously taken up Solzhenitsyn's challenge to "Live Not by Lies!"—citing the 1974 essay as an inspiration on more than a few occasions. In a striking essay in the November 2021 issue of *Commentary*,[4] Weiss highlights the intimate connection in our new situation between courage and the "unqualified rejection of lies." In the spirit of Solzhenitsyn, she impressively outlines the categorical imperative underlying the rejection of woke despotism as all forms of ideological despotism: "Do not speak untruths, either about yourself or anyone else, no matter the comfort offered by the mob." She gives multiple inspiring examples of Americans—professors, teachers, lawyers, parents—who are doing precisely that with courage and moral integrity. Inspired by Solzhenitsyn, Weiss has a sturdy confidence that in the right circumstances "courage can be contagious." About that she is surely right.

In his book *Live Not by Lies*, published in 2020, the Orthodox Christian and conservative culture critic Rod Dreher draws wisely on Solzhenitsyn's appeal to civic courage and spiritual integrity with special emphasis on the threat to religious liberty and traditional morality posed by the woke revolutionaries. His thoughtful and provocative book has sold well over two hundred thousand copies despite a de-facto media embargo by such publications as *The New York Times*, who used to cover his books in a vigorous and respectful way.

Then there is the equally inspiring story of the musician Winston Marshall of the world-famous band Mumford and Sons. Under immense pressure from a censorious Twitter mob for retweeting an account of brutal Antifa violence in Portland, Oregon, he quit the band—he did not want the group to feel permanent pressure from a mob whose ferociousness refused to give way—but forswore to back off or apologize for perfectly honorable convictions. Inspired by the peroration of Solzhenitsyn's "Live Not by Lies!," a text that fortified his will and gave him encouragement and strength, Marshall remained true to his convictions (see his impressive interview with Bari Weiss in *The Free Press*, July 1, 2021). Between the mob and his "sense of integrity," he chose the latter. This is civic courage that inspires and reinvigorates the soul.

[38]

We do not want to overstate. Since free institutions are not yet moribund in the United States, not yet at least, one would like to believe that this counterrevolution that Solzhenitsyn has helped instigate has more than a fighting chance at succeeding. Let us do our best to make this reasonable hope come true. But short of ultimate success, what matters first and foremost is maintaining the integrity of our souls.

The Choice and Challenge before Us

As I have argued elsewhere, the categorical rejection of the Ideological Lie is the precondition for the next crucial step of civic salvation: building a "parallel polis," to borrow a term from Václav Benda, a series of parallel institutions that reject the hate-filled lies at the heart of every tyrannical and ideological project that has deformed the late modern world. Benda, the Czech-Catholic dissident from the period of his country's Communist captivity, wrote with great luminosity and insight about the need to create a parallel polis. Benda was dealing with a full-fledged totalitarian state where oppression came from on high and seemingly obliterated any possibility of a true civil society. As Benda wrote in the second of two famous essays on the parallel polis, existential resistance to the suffocating Ideological Lie must (and had already) given rise to new civic initiatives, however harried and repressed, that went beyond the natural or existential "resistance of life to totalitarianism."[5] There must be a "deliberate expansion of the space in which the parallel polis can exist." The "killing winds of totalitarianism," as Benda called them, will strike at these initiatives with all their force—but new institutions and initiatives will emerge in response, and the forces of totalitarianism will gradually become demoralized as "new territory" is conquered by the forces of liberty and human dignity. So was Benda's hope, one that turned out to be vindicated in the annus mirabilis that was 1989 that eliminated Communist rule (and Soviet domination) in east-central Europe.

The analogy to our current situation is inexact since our despotism comes largely, if not exclusively, from forces *within* civil society (and with the angry Twitter mobs and university activists as their sansculottes). But

[39]

the rise of Substack as a source of independent journalism and intellectual resistance by leading voices on the right, center, and independent left provides an imitable model of how to outmaneuver the forces of repression. (As we have just noted, an honest, courageous, and independent liberal, Bari Weiss, is helping to show the way.) New universities and classical schools are no doubt needed since accreditation agencies at every level are committed to locking in the culture of repudiation and the new religion of diversity and inclusion (misnamed "equity") in perpetuity. Groups like the Intercollegiate Studies Institute, under the energetic leadership of Johnny Burtka, now rightly see their role as providing the education in citizenship, statesmanship, classical political economy, and the Western classics that are more or less crowded out of mainstream institutions of higher learning. Hillsdale College provides a practicable model, as does its Barney Charter School Initiative, which helps create and support independent classical academies. And the admirable efforts of Heterodox Academy, founded by the politically unclassifiable psychologist Jonathan Haidt in 2015 to defend the place of viewpoint diversity and "constructive disagreement in institutions of higher learning," as their mission statement puts it, are more important than ever. The new state-mandated institutes in more than thirteen "red" and "purple" states dedicated to the teaching and study of "civic thought" and founding principles are also a promising sign of hope and resistance.[6]

Let me add the caveat: Only institutions that self-consciously reject woke assumptions in the name of truth and liberty are likely to maintain their integrity and autonomy. The building and sustaining of such institutions—classical schools, new universities dedicated to enduring truths and the old civilities, institutes dedicated to the study of citizenship and statesmanship—is more and more in evidence and must be supported by all people of good will. But one must begin at the beginning—the personal decision not to live by lies. From that wise and liberating decision, all else will flow.

All that is asked of us is to display moral integrity and a modicum of civic spirit. If we reject this path, we surely deserve the scorn owed

Pushkin's passive and contemptuous herd of cattle who are all too content with their enslavement. The choice—so momentous with consequence—is truly our own. The loss of civic and intellectual freedom is neither preordained nor inevitable. The future is not written in advance, and self-respecting human persons, informed by free will and moral conscience, are never obliged to surrender to "fatality."

Sources and Suggested Readings

MARTIN MALIA's aptly named *The Soviet Tragedy: A History of Socialism in Russia, 1917–1991* (New York: Free Press, 1995) remains the most incisive historical critique of Soviet ideocracy ever written. To his credit, Malia saw Communist ideology as a phantom or farce that could only culminate in tyranny, terror, mendacity, and economic penury—in a word: tragedy on a massive scale.

FOR THE DISCUSSION of ideology's essential role in amplifying tyranny and violence on a truly unprecedented scale, see the chapter "The Bluecaps" in the authorized abridgement of Solzhenitsyn's *The Gulag Archipelago* (New York: Vintage Classics, 2023), 75–78.

IN *Live Not by Lies: A Manual for Christian Dissidents* (New York: Sentinel, 2020), Rod Dreher draws on Solzhenitsyn's famous 1974 manifesto to highlight the necessity for all those who adhere to the old religion and the old morality (and people of good will more generally) to muster courage and uncompromising moral integrity in resisting the encroachments of woke despotism.

CHAPTER 4

POSTCOLONIAL IDEOLOGY
AND ITS DISCONTENTS

PART I

Wretched of the University

LET US RETURN to the summer of 2020, when decent Americans found themselves overcome by a torrent of propaganda besmirching the United States as a nation racist to its core, with "white privilege" making life intolerable for anyone but its immediate beneficiaries. A fanatical moralism demanded that all correct-thinking people sign on to an antiracist catechism that was as simplistic as it was absurd. And plead "guilty" untold numbers of people did, with a whiff of the Chinese Cultural Revolution in the air.

Civic courage was hardly to be found, and accommodation to ready-made lies provided a momentary reprieve for those, especially on the left, afraid of being "canceled" by their censorious peers utilizing social media as the weapon most ready-at-hand. The ritualistic self-loathing that had long been present, even institutionalized, on college campuses became the norm in journalism, the entertainment business, corporate culture, professional sports, and in many churches and synagogues, too.

As we have already discussed in chapter 1, naïve liberals and suburban housewives joined the hardened Marxists and Maoists (and grifters, too) of Black Lives Matter in demanding the radical revolutionary transformation of a country still largely free, decent, and self-critical. The police became targets of angry mobs (and Antifa terrorists), and pressure grew to withdraw police protection from the weak, aged, and vulnerable, especially in minority communities.

The revolution was driven in large part by white progressives, trust-fund babies, and the like who marched as they bandied about tired and stale slogans. In the name of "antiracism," whole groups of people were stigmatized for belonging to the wrong race or "gender," an ugly and now-ubiquitous word that has become meaningless as it has been weaponized. Everything was racialized, and it became verboten to judge people by the "content of their character," in Martin Luther King's famous words. Those blacks, not a few in number, who wanted to think for themselves, who refused to define themselves as helpless victims and nothing else, were subject to vituperation. The loud, the angry, the uncivil, and the massively uninformed were lauded for their so-called courage and social consciousness. For months, the most "privileged" Americans playacted at revolution, as if any ideological revolution can ever end well.

For all intents and purposes, America had a collective nervous breakdown. Grown-ups took their bearings from eighteen-year-olds repeating mindless and extremist slogans (and finding "systematic" violence and mass killings against black Americans where they didn't exist). In their "socially constructed" world, an ideological Second Reality competed with the common world where citizens debate and deliberate, sometimes contentiously but never violently, about matters of public import.

Racializing woke activists clearly did not believe in civic deliberation. Instead, they felt perfectly entitled to threaten, intimidate, and silence those who would not freely assent to their ideological nostrums. Notice how unpopular free speech—and the First Amendment—are among those who have left the world of constitutional democracy behind. Like the totalitarians of old, they believe in fiat—binding commands—and the triumph of the will rather than the arts of republican persuasion. Lastly, as we have stressed, their racial Manichæism, their simplistic and arbitrary division of the world into evil exploiters and innocent victims, leaves no place for moral responsibility, civic reconciliation, and true justice, racial or otherwise.

Since Hamas's cruel and sadistic attacks in southern Israel on October 7, 2023, we have seen yet another academic-induced outburst of ideological insanity, one that is truly bewildering to much of the public. In the summer of 2020, many decent Americans discovered for the first time (how could that be?) that their children had been indoctrinated for untold years in a cult of racialist victimization and recrimination that denied the very legitimacy of America's founding principles and the nation's capacity for civic and moral self-correction. The 1619 Project (to be discussed in chapter 9), a house of cards built on a mountain of lies, was the perfect illustration of racialist self-righteousness that damned America in a misbegotten attempt to purify it. Washington, Lincoln, and Frederick Douglass had to go so that Ibram X. Kendi (né Henry Rogers) and Nikole Hannah-Jones could transform our land of hope into a bastion of despair and racial enmity. In a wokified America, one wins Pulitzer Prizes for such crude and strident efforts at civic division and subversion.

Now, Americans witness campus activists cheering on the unconscionable nihilists of Hamas as if they were bona-fide freedom fighters. LGBTQ++ activists cheer militants who would surely execute them in a matter of minutes. A considerable number of activists, professors, and left-wing students compare Israel and Zionism (the great ongoing project to give nationhood to the Jewish people) to apartheid at best and Nazism at worst. University presidents at MIT, Harvard, and UPenn, among others, suddenly rediscovered free speech—so long as that speech was deployed to hate and harass Jews with impunity. They seem confident they can get away with such transparent dishonesty. Students scream genocidal slogans ("From the river to the sea"), displaying unabashed sympathy for the murderous intent of the slogan but palpable ignorance of what river and what sea they are referring to. The obvious responsibility of Hamas, a brutally thuggish embodiment of Islamist fanaticism, for the war that inevitably followed the October 7 attacks, and their clear desire to exacerbate civilian casualties, are all but ignored.

For the hard Left and their more sentimental fellow travelers, there are never any differences between war and war crimes. By their criteria every act of resistance to a genocidal foe is in fact genocidal. Pacifism is the only just response to terrorism by those who hate the dreaded

Western world. This logic is hardly impeccable or morally admirable.

The Israelis who built modern Jerusalem and made the desert bloom (much to the surprise and admiration of King Abdullah of Jordan, who was shot by a Palestinian extremist in 1951 for his failure to hate Israel enough) are reduced in the new vulgate to Nazis attempting to create *Lebensraum* for themselves. The Israelis did not ignite the war with the Arab League in 1948 that, for all intents and purposes, destroyed the prospects for a Palestinian state, which would have been the first one in history. After 1948, while Israel took in well over a million Jews from both Europe and the broad Arab Islamic world (where they faced discrimination at best and repression at worst), building housing for them and incorporating them into the nascent Jewish state, Arab leaders let those Palestinians who had fled Israel during or before the 1948 war sink into refugee camps where they and their descendants remain to this day. It was a cruel, cynical move, and one that was demagogic and irresponsible to its core.

What the Middle East saw in 1948 to 1950 was a mass population exchange like the one that occurred between Turkey and Greece in the early 1920s. Responsible people know there is no going back on this exchange (on all this see Martin Gilbert's excellent *Israel: A History*, last updated in 2008). The least that can be said is that the activists, students, professors, and administrators who deny the moral and political legitimacy of the state of Israel inhabit a fact-free zone where ideology and invective replace both empirical realities and the judicious exercise of political reason.

The new anti-Semitism is much more than anti-Semitism. Age-old anti-Semitism is a very real but subordinate phenomenon. Today, what comes first is Western self-loathing, the obscene conviction that the Western world, and it alone, is the source of colonialism, slavery, racism, injustice, totalitarianism, and economic exploitation. Postcolonial discourse, as mendacious as its "antiracist" twin, is now omnipresent in academic and intellectual circles. It corrupts minds and rewrites history in mind-boggling ways. In English and Comparative Literature departments, it has largely displaced the humane and sympathetic engagement with literary classics.

In the sections to follow, I will dissect postcolonialism, a mode of analysis and argumentation that rivals Jacobinism and Bolshevism for its valorization of violence, its systematic distortion of the past, and its division of the world into evil exploiters and innocent victims, a terrible simplification, indeed. It is postcolonial discourse that has played such a major role in turning the citizens of a democratic Jewish state into contemporary, if imaginary, Nazis in the minds of the woke. And along the way, I will have the temerity to ask if the British Empire, for example, was truly the unmitigated evil that the postcolonialists insist it was.

PART II

The Delusions of Postcolonial Ideology

Come, fix upon me that accusing eye.
I thirst for accusation.

—W.B. YEATS, "Parnell's Funeral"

THUS BEGAN the seminal 1976 article "Western Guilt & Third World Poverty," first published in *Commentary* by the great developmental economist P. T. Bauer and then reproduced in an expanded version in his 1981 book, *Equality, the Third World, and Economic Delusion*.[1] That book was published by Harvard University Press, something that could probably not happen today. Bauer, a refugee from Hungary and a professor for many decades at the London School of Economics, was the scourge of postcolonial discourse well before it received a name and became a suffocating orthodoxy in Western academic and intellectual circles. He remains among the surest guides to thinking seriously about questions that are now dominated by ideological clichés with little or no basis in fact.

In his essay, Bauer pointed out that the "poorest and most backward countries have until recently had no external economic contacts and often have never been Western colonies" (*ETWED*, 67). He took aim at the widespread sophistry that the prosperity of Western democracies depended upon the past and present exploitation of various African, Asian, and Latin American colonies and dependencies. Responding to a typical argument excoriating the British for taking the "rubber from Malaya, the tea from India, [and] raw materials from all over the world" and giving "almost nothing in return," Bauer highlighted the inconvenient truth that the British "took the rubber *to* Malaya and the tea *to* India" (*ETWED*, 67).

Truth be told, before the Western presence in these countries, there was little or no "wealth to be drained" (*ETWED*, 68–69). Famines occurred quite frequently in countries that had no significant political or economic contact with Western countries. While untold numbers of intellectuals, academics, and activists specialize, then and now, in blaming the West for Third World poverty in its various forms, Bauer highlighted a truth far more ignored than acknowledged:

> So far from condemning Third World people to death, Western contacts have been behind the large increase in life expectation in the Third World, so often deplored as the population explosion by the same critics (ETWED, 68).

Bauer admired the ability of ordinary people to better their lot and live in dignity when common sense, the rule of law, and economic sanity prevailed in developing countries. He cheered the success of the "Asian Tigers" (e.g., Taiwan, Singapore, South Korea, and pre-1997 Hong Kong), whose remarkable economic and political transformations disproved the radical pessimism and insistent nihilism of para-Marxist dependency theory. Quite simply, the success of these countries had nothing to do with cutting themselves off from international markets or private enterprise and economic competition.

In contrast, African and Latin American leaders who took their bearings from fashionable Western theories rooted in guilt and collectivist assumptions brought tyranny and penury to their countries. The then-famous and fashionable Kwame Nkrumah impoverished the once-prosperous Gold Coast (now Ghana). Countless tyrants and demagogues, such as Robert Mugabe in Zimbabwe and the Marxist-Leninist Mengistu Haile Mariam in Ethiopia, rapidly undid what progress had been made in their respective countries.

And how strange it is that apologists for the Communist dictatorship in Cuba blame that country's self-induced problems—in 1959 it was the fourth most prosperous country in the Americas with a thriving middle class—on an American economic embargo that has kept that island from being a full participant in capitalist world markets? Even Cuba's Communist tyrants know that socialist autarky (or the radical economic self-sufficiency advocated by Marxist theory) is in truth an invitation to disaster.

Bauer recounted how the West opened up much of the Third World to the invigorating presence of the Chinese, Indians, and Levantines (*ETWED*, 73). These entrepreneurs and economic middlemen who thrived outside their own countries were sources of economic dynamism, vitality, and prosperity. When Third World tyrants turned on them, as the murderous and insane Idi Amin did in Uganda in 1973 by expelling them from the country, calamity almost immediately ensued.

P. T. Bauer also appreciated how remarkably immune to evidence postcolonial ideology turned out to be. As the West became more prosperous after abandoning the various European empires—English, French, Dutch, and Belgian—ideologues took aim at an allegedly ubiquitous network of "neocolonialism." Contact with the West was said to be the source of almost all evils, and local tyrants and self-aggrandizing and corrupt elites were given a free pass when not celebrated as "liberators" and "freedom fighters."

In contrast, Bauer placed blame on the West for entirely different reasons. To be sure, empire and colonialism were not without moral and political fault. But in the decades during and after decolonialization, the "development" policies of Western elites and international organizations served to "politicize economic life in the Third World." (*ETWED*, 83) "A ready-made framework for state-controlled economies or even for totalitarian states was presented to the incoming governments" (*ETWED*, 83), Bauer noted.

Corruption on a mass scale was an inevitable byproduct of replacing limited government under British colonial rule with statist regimes and elites unscrupulously fighting over the trough created by Western aid. Discrimination and persecution of successful ethnic minorities allowed corrupt and despotic governments to curry favor with the disempowered population at large. The ill-advised efforts inspired by Western guilt thus paradoxically benefited kleptocratic elites and hurt those individuals and groups struggling to improve their lot in life through hard work, acquired skills, and enterprise rather than unscrupulously raiding the political and economic commons.

Finally, Bauer understood just how much what has come to be called postcolonial ideology drew on pathological Western self-loathing, a debilitating guilt that undermines the moral legitimacy of Western civilization while doing immense damage to the prospects of the countries relegated to the so-called Third World. In all these ways, his groundbreaking work helps us today better appreciate how many of the regnant assumptions about colonialism, Western guilt, and Third World "oppression" and poverty exist in a fact-free zone dominated by accusatory ideological clichés.

This becomes even more apparent through a reading of Thomas Sowell's encyclopedic *Conquests and Cultures*.[2] With his typical mixture of empiricism and good sense, Sowell demonstrates just how ubiquitous war, conquests, and slavery have been in the human experience. To see these as monopolies of a uniquely oppressive and culpable West is simply absurd.

Without cultural "appropriation" and the ongoing interpenetration of peoples, the experience of human beings would be terribly impoverished, as Sowell's opening discussion of the shaping of British character, history, politics, and economics throughout the ages makes abundantly clear (*CC*, 22–30). Sowell is perfectly up front about the West's own crimes and misdeeds, as any honest scholar and citizen ought to be. But he also tells the story of the eighteen million victims of the cruel Islamic slave trade with its mountain of cadavers, eunuchs, and a marked condescension (or worse) toward all things African (*CC*, 153–57).

Sowell passes over neither the crimes of the conquistadors nor the human sacrifices and cannibalism of the Aztecs and the cruel despotism of the Incans (*CC*, 267–69). There were many predations committed by colonizers in Spanish America (*CC*, 277–81, 285–89). But there were also numerous popes who denounced the cruelties and iniquities of slavery and the slave trade. Men such as the sixteenth-century Spanish priest Bartolemé de las Casas fiercely denounced injustices against native peoples and pleaded for the cause of common humanity (*CC*, 269–70).

In England, inspired by the dual legacies of Christianity and the mutually reinforcing doctrines of natural rights and law, public opinion turned dramatically against slavery. After 1833 and for most of the nineteenth century, the British Navy became one of the great global instruments for expanding human rights through extirpating the slave trade. It did so with zeal and efficiency. Such calibrated self-criticism is part and parcel of authentic national honor and self-respect.

What stands out, despite everything, is the West's salutary capacity for self-criticism and self-correction, traits far from abundant in the rest of the world.

"Enough of pesky facts!" the angry moralists and ideologues will cry. What of "systemic injustice" and the "intrinsic evil" of one people ruling another people against their will? In the next section of this chapter, we will turn to *Colonialism*, the recent book by the Oxford theologian and social ethicist Nigel Biggar, who provides a model of moral seriousness on this most contested of issues. With his help, and that of others, we will also show that postcolonial ideology is itself very much in need of a moral reckoning. As the French social theorist René Girard argued at the end of his life, untold damage has been done to moral judgment

[51]

and political prudence by a "caricatural 'ultra-Christianity' that tries to escape from the Judeo-Christian orbit by 'radicalizing' the concerns for victims in an anti-Christian manner."[3]

Whatever happened, we will ask, to a sober recognition of original sin, shared moral accountability, and turning the sword inward before doing so outward? There lies the real thing, Christian realism, and not its pernicious caricature, postcolonial ideology. We will also show that moral judgment must be based in a scrupulous attentiveness to empirical realities and to the wellsprings of human nature. Otherwise, it becomes mere sentimentality, at best, or, at worst, a weapon in the hands of extremists and ideologues.

PART III

Self-Loathing as Self-Righteousness: The Paradoxical Perversities of Postcolonial Ideology

POSTCOLONIALISM, AS we have already made abundantly clear, has nothing to do with a disinterested inquiry into the truth, or even a fair-minded evaluation of the strengths and weaknesses of the West's dynamic, but imperfect, civilization. Rather it is an ideological current that delights in denying any moral legitimacy to the most self-critical civilization in human history, an approach in which history is weaponized and distorted beyond all recognition. As the French political philosopher Pierre Manent has suggested, if apolitical humanitarianism is a perversion of charity, then wokeness, which animates postcolonialism, perverts the Christian call to repentance. In a world without original sin, some are said to be ontologically guilty and beyond redemption, and others, those deigned victims, are shorn of moral agency and remain forever "innocent" as if in some idyllic prelapsarian state. At the center of this perverse parody of old Christian truths and virtues is the pathological self-loathing that we began to analyze in the first two sections of this chapter.

A most welcome intellectual antidote to this ideologization of historical inquiry, guilt, and judgment can be found in a recent, widely discussed book by Nigel Biggar entitled *Colonialism: A Moral Reckoning*, published by William Collins in 2023.[4] Bloomsbury, his original publisher, refused to publish the book after an academic/activist mob descended on it. Without reviewing the book, I will identify some of its principal insights while providing illustrations and insights of my own.

Biggar, a Christian realist of the Niebuhrian type, never confuses moral judgment with moralistic fanaticism or facile and predictable condemnations. He follows the Nigerian novelist Chinua Achebe, the author of the acclaimed 1958 novel *Things Fall Apart*, who shortly before his death in 2013 told an Iranian journalist that the "legacy of colonialism is not a simple one but one of great complexity, with contradictions—good things as well as bad."[5] Achebe strongly opposed colonialism per se, in large part because it made of the native population "some kind of ward or minor requiring protection." But he admired the good work of Christian missionaries who provided him and his father with fine educations, and he noted with appreciation the relative absence of corruption in the British colonial administration. The contrast with postindependence Nigeria could not be any more striking, he observed (*CAMR*, 89–90, 197, 199–200).

A reader of Biggar's book will learn that Canada's loathed residential schools for the native population were hardly hellholes and did much good in training and educating young Indians. They sometimes went too far in discouraging the study of native languages and native religious traditions, though as Christian clergy, they could hardly be faulted for taking the Great Commission seriously. Charges of "cultural genocide" against them are hyperbolic, to say the least (*CAMR*, 127–35). Biggar ably demonstrates how forced the contemporary identification of racism, slavery, and colonialism really are. To be sure, he is sensitive, as any decent person must be, to the terrible cruelties of the Atlantic slave trade (even if—one of the many important points of the book—the West had no monopoly on the evils associated with slavery and the slave trade).

In his book we meet, in his own words, "brutal slavery, the epidemic spread of devastating disease, economic and social disruption; the unjust displacement of natives by settlers; elements of racial alienation and racial contempt" and more (*CAMR*, 276). But, at the same time, the British were a comparatively humane colonial power and "in the history of the British Empire, there was nothing morally comparable to Nazi concentration or death camps, or to the Soviet Gulag" (*CAMR*, 276). Moreover, there were powerful countervailing tendencies that need to be taken into account, including the massive campaign that Britain and her navy waged against the international slave trade for most of the nineteenth century in the years after 1833. In that admirable and sustained effort to unite "justice and force," in Pascal's memorable and suggestive phrase, the British did themselves proud.

Lord Palmerston took particular satisfaction in the role that he and the British government played in forcing Brazil to end the slave trade in a country where slavery was at once the most brutal and deadly (*CAMR*, 59). Christian morality (think of William Wilberforce's long and ultimately successful struggle against slavery and the slave trade) and liberal principles increasingly influenced British policy, and both for the good. Biggar even rescues the reputation of the much-derided Cecil Rhodes—colonialist, mining magnate, and adventurer par excellence. Rhodes never denied the common humanity shared by blacks and whites, and he supported suffrage for blacks and mixed-race persons in South Africa who met certain educational and property requirements. Many of the hideously racist sentiments (and quotations) attributed to Rhodes by hostile biographers and activists have been made up whole cloth and then endlessly recycled by even more hostile activists (on Rhodes, see *CAMR*, 2–3, 69, 71, 72, 73–74). Predictably, truth is the first victim of ideologically inspired historiography.

Some Telling Counterexamples

Let me add some examples of my own to show that the ritualistic identification of empire with slavery and racism is far more ideological

sloganeering than measured political and historical analysis. The coun-
terexamples are abundant and instructive. Edmund Burke, the great
Anglo-Irish parliamentarian and political philosopher, despised slavery
and wrote "A Sketch of the Negro Code" in 1780 in order to lay out a
workable plan for gradual emancipation. He loathed Warren Hastings's
heavy-handed direction of the East India Company, accusing the governor general of corruption and cruel disdain for long-established Indian
customs. Hastings and the East India Company, Burke suggested, ruled
India like a rapacious, conquering army. Burke spent twelve years fiercely pursuing an ultimately failed impeachment of Hastings.

Burke also took pointed aim at the anti-Catholic penal laws in Ireland
and argued that the majority Catholic population needed to be brought
into the political community, their rights respected, and their interests
represented (at least partially), in the Irish parliament. It is true that
Burke never condemned empire per se. But he worked for an empire
whose spirit was humane and magnanimous, rather than heavy-handed
and dominated by self-aggrandizement and a petty concern for lucre.
As such, he was a partisan of civilized and civilizing empire, however
contradictory that might seem to our contemporary postcolonialists.
For them, condemnation and self-loathing are the alpha and omega of
postcolonial discourse and ideology. They desperately need to expand
their moral and historical imaginations.

Alexis de Tocqueville favored the French conquest of Algeria, even as
he vigorously fought slavery at home and abroad. In 1855, he wrote an
open letter to Americans, published in the abolitionist journal *Liberty
Bell*, expressing his unease at "seeing Slavery retard" America's "progress,
tarnish her glory, furnish arms to her detractors, [and] compromise the
future career of the Union."[6] He spoke about being deeply "moved at the
spectacle of man's degradation by man." A supporter of civilized empire,
Tocqueville detested both slavery and racism and opposed any effort
to forcibly convert Algerians to Christianity from Islam (even though
he thought the "fatalism" of Islam deterred social progress and was in
the end detrimental to robust intellectual and political freedoms). The

[55]

terrible simplifications of the postcolonial ideologues cannot begin to do justice to the complex judgments and moral bearing of a thinker and statesman such as Tocqueville.

For his part, the great Winston Churchill fiercely opposed the precipitous granting of independence to the peoples of the Indian subcontinent. But his motives were hardly racist. He feared that Hindus and Muslims might butcher each other if the British were no longer there to moderate and arbitrate their respective communal demands. (In the event, Partition was attended by mass violence and wholesale human slaughter in 1947 and 1948.) Churchill did not want Britain to be responsible for unleashing "primordial chaos" in a country for which she had long had responsibility. In a 1931 speech, he took aim at India's Brahman elite who, he said, prattled on about the "Rights of Man" even as they ignored and belittled India's long-suffering "untouchables."[7] In that same speech, he even suggested that if Christ were to come back to earth, he might first go to minister to the "untouchables of India" in order "to give them the tidings that not only are all men equal in the sight of God, but that for the weak and the poor and downtrodden a double blessing is reserved."[8] This is hardly the voice of an advocate of genocide, cultural or otherwise.

Today, the fevered Left (and those too ignorant or cowardly to stand up to them) dismiss Churchill as an imperialist and worse. They quote him selectively and confuse a defense of empire with a bent for cruelty, exploitation, and even genocide. But Churchill was not so crude. After panicked British troops opened fire on unarmed Indians in Amritsar in 1919, Churchill condemned the massacre unequivocally and forcefully. He spoke, echoing Macaulay, of the "most frightful of all spectacles, the strength of 'civilization without its mercy.'" Here magnanimity meets humility in a truly admirable way. The overwrought, unreflective presentism of our academic and ideological elites gets in the way of anything resembling equitable historical and moral analysis and judgment.

A Balanced Judgment from the East

Unlike the array of postcolonialists who mercilessly condemn the West and deny its moral legitimacy (and thus, in the end, its right to exist), Biggar points out that in July 2005, India's then–Prime Minister Manmohan Singh, in a speech at the University of Oxford weighing the credits and debits of British colonial rule in his native country, generously acknowledged the "beneficial consequences" of British rule in India, including rule of law, constitutional government, a professional civil service, and modern universities and research centers. He tellingly added: "Our constitution remains a testimony to the enduring interplay between what is essentially Indian and what is very British in our intellectual heritage" (*CAMR*, 283–84).

The postcolonialists are incapable of sharing Singh's equanimity and balanced judgment. As Biggar puts it, their "exaggeration of colonialism's sins is often not at all reluctant, but willful, even gleeful" (*CAMR*, 295). Theirs is a nihilistic inversion of Christianity, a perverse "anti-Christian Christianity" as René Girard has called it, where the West can do nothing right and the "Other" can do no wrong. In their self-understanding, the West remains at the center of world history but as the Evil Empire, the pariah to be canceled and excluded until the end of the world.

Self-Hatred as a Weapon

"There is a self-obsessive quality to this attitude" Biggar notes (*CAMR*, 296). For his part, Biggar worries that the continued inculcation of nihilism as perverse self-righteousness will continue to undermine the self-confidence of those trusted to preserve a liberal international order friendly to humane Western values (*CAMR*, 296–97). But perhaps that particular train has already left the station. Instead, self-abnegation already plays a crucial role in an emerging woke imperium where democracies fight an ill-defined racism and promote LGBTQ+ ideology, and where the Christian principles that led free peoples to take on slavery and the slave trade are mocked as incompatible with modern "freedom."

Postcolonialism, alas, is already a defining feature of the public philosophy, the ruling ideology, of progressives everywhere in the Western world. That, alas, does not bode well for historical truth or the future of Western liberty. That is why this latest ideological manifestation of Western self-hatred must be truthfully and manfully resisted.

Sources and Suggested Readings

THE BAUER, Sowell, and Biggar volumes already cited in the body of the text provide admirable models for addressing the issue of colonialism in an empirically grounded and morally serious way, freed from regnant ideological posturing and the tyranny of clichés.

MY DISCUSSION of Israel and its admirable efforts to take in millions of displaced European and Arab Jews after 1948 draws on Marin Gilbert, *Israel: A History* (New York: Harper Perennial, 2008). See page 274 for the discussion of King Abdullah's admiration for the Zionist achievement.

SEE DANIEL J. MAHONEY, *The Statesman as Thinker: Portraits of Greatness, Courage and Moderation* (New York: Encounter Books, 2002) for a discussion of the humane and calibrated position of Burke, Tocqueville, and Churchill on the morality of empire.

CHAPTER 5

"VIRTUE AND TERROR": ROBESPIERRE AND HIS NEW APOLOGISTS

THE HISTORY OF ideology is inseparable from the bottomless self-radicalization of the French Revolution and its evolution from 1789 to 1793. Maximilien Robespierre is far from yesterday's news. In important respects, his paradoxes reveal the paradoxes that remain at the heart of a powerful and deformed version of modernity: a maximalist approach to rights that gives rise to implacable tyranny; a constant search for enemies and conspirators who inevitably fail the test of revolutionary purity; an absolute confidence in the "people" that is compatible with unprecedented forms of repression; the self-obsession of those on "the right side of History" who never question their own motives or acknowledge their own imperfections. In the end, political "Virtue" as annunciated by Robespierre had Terror as its necessary instrument and accompaniment, with the regime of the "Rights of Man" culminating in rivers of blood. How could such a man, and such a lurid approach to modern politics, continue to divide us?

In *Robespierre: The Man Who Divides Us the Most,*[1] recently published in translation by Princeton University Press, the distinguished contemporary French political philosopher Marcel Gauchet (less well-known in the Anglophone world than he should be) speaks of a "division" that above all characterizes French opinion about Robespierre and Jacobinism (R, 1–8). The latter was the most radical and consistent of the major factions among the French Revolutionaries from 1789 onward. But as we shall see, Robespierre and the Jacobins have their contemporary partisans—and even imitators—outside of France, too. For Robespierre is no ordinary tyrant, no man of unhinged ambition striving for power at any cost. In the early years of the Revolution,

Robespierre spoke of nothing but the "Rights of Man," of popular government, and the need to eschew any compromise with the remnants of the ancien régime. In his view of things, before 1789 one sees only tyranny, darkness, and oppression; on the other side of the chronological divide there is liberty, emancipation, and the dawn of the reign of the "Rights of Man." But the transition required rivers of blood to flow. The killing machine that Robespierre became is inseparable from his uncompromising dedication to the "Rights of Man." The "hero" and the "monster" are one and the same man, fanatically dedicated to the same principles (R, 6, 168–71). This ought to give us pause.

Gauchet attempts, and largely succeeds, in doing justice to both sides of the equation. He thus avoids painting Robespierre simply in black. In the end, however, with a different rhetorical emphasis to be sure, Gauchet arrives at a position not all that distinct from that of his friend and predecessor, the great historian of the French Revolution François Furet: the Terror is no mere aberration but has seeds in 1789. The absolutism inherent in the French Revolution is rooted in its extreme valorization of rights without due consideration of prudential considerations or the practical and demanding requirements of "orderly government," a theme at the center of Gauchet's book (R, 3). This is connected to the ease with which the revolutionaries dispensed with what Raymond Aron liked to call the "wisdom of Montesquieu," the sober and sobering recognition that all power needs to be limited and constrained. The opposite has roots in revolutionary ideology itself. If Furet announces his conclusion at the beginning of his investigation, taking pointed aim at the "revolutionary catechism" that had distorted the study of the French Revolution for a century or more, Gauchet arrives at similar conclusions more slowly, prudently, and with greater hesitation.

The differences between Furet and Gauchet thus are more rhetorical than substantive, with different emphases on the way to similar conclusions. But Gauchet's caution and restraint has the paradoxical advantage of allowing us to see how essential features of liberalism and liberal "ideology"—reducing the political problem to the protection of the rights of man, and even the categories of democracy and representation—can take a decidedly despotic, even totalitarian, turn. This is a truth highlighted much earlier by French counterrevolutionaries such as Joseph de Maistre and Louis de Bonald, and in a different way by liberals such as Benjamin Constant, François Guizot, and Alexis de Tocqueville. But it is largely forgotten by contemporary historians—who are at once too empiricist (lost in minutiae) and ideological (uncritical as they are of the "emancipatory" aims of the French Revolution)—and by ideological activists who want to change the world, come what may.

Gauchet's judicious mixture of erudition and moderation illumines what is at stake in the figure of Robespierre, while avoiding undue polemics. Rather than trumpeting the connections between the rights of man and revolutionary atrocities, he allows the links between hero and monster to reveal themselves through careful analyses of Robespierre's speech and deed. The public Robespierre, who came increasingly to the forefront between the spring of 1789 and his demise on the ninth of Thermidor Year II (July 27, 1794), is above all to be grasped through the words that poured forth from his mouth in the National Assembly and the National Convention. In them, he presented himself as the exemplary defender of revolutionary principles, the "virtuous" representative of the people, and the scourge of the revolution's enemies, real and imagined (by the end, they were promiscuously imagined). Gauchet underscores Robespierre's "disposition to impersonality," a talent for self-abnegation that allowed him to identify himself wholly and unreservedly with the revolutionary cause (R, 186). (Lenin would display this same mixture of totalitarian will and austere "impersonality.") But his "noble cause," as he undoubtedly perceived it, was fully compatible with fanaticism and an unreasonable belief in his absolute moral rectitude.

Gauchet suggestively argues that Robespierre came to see himself as the "divine man" alluded to by Rousseau in his *Social Contract* (R, 169–70). Over time, Gauchet argues, a "craving for popularity took root in him and flourished" (R, 50). Robespierre, like all of us, was human, all too human. He saw in criticism directed at him only counterrevolutionary

[61]

malice at work and could thus abandon such old friends as Camille Desmoulins to the ferocity of the revolutionary mob, if such abandonment was demanded by revolutionary rectitude (*R*, 108, 112–13). "The Incorruptible," as the ascetic Robespierre was called, was not immune to an inhuman ideological cruelty. Indeed, he embodied it. Montesquieu wrote in *The Spirit of the Laws* (Book XI, chapter 4) that "virtue," by which he primarily meant *political* virtue, "itself has need of limits." Robespierre and his Jacobin cohorts perfectly illustrate Montesquieu's point. For that alone, Robespierre will remain a living presence in universal history, a permanent reminder of what must be avoided for the sake of a political community marked by liberty and moderation.

The same Robespierre who saw enemies everywhere (one of his most memorable speeches is called "Les Ennemis de la Patrie démasqués") ferociously dedicated himself to defending revolutionary principles. These at first appear to be uncontroversial and even choice-worthy liberal principles. The French ideologue defended freedom of speech, representative government, and the right to property, and he lambasted the death penalty as both immoral and ineffective. On the last point, he was one with Cesare Beccaria, who himself drew on Hobbes's account of self-preservation as the foundational political principle. In the years between 1789 and 1791, Robespierre did not initially oppose the monarchy as such (*R*, 40–42). But he fiercely denounced a royal veto (even of a temporary kind) as a concession to tyranny and completely at odds with the requirements of the "general will," whose will he conflated with his own.

Robespierre's "liberalism," if we can call it that, was decidedly marred by its rejection of the "wisdom of Montesquieu" and the tyrant's increasing identification of himself with the purity of revolutionary principles. Gauchet tellingly calls one of his chapters "I, the People" (*R*, 34–58). Robespierre began to divinize himself because he divinized the revolutionary people. After Louis XVI's flight to Varennes in June 1791, Robespierre and the Jacobins attacked the king with inhuman ferocity. Robespierre told the Convention that the king is *by definition* a tyrant and that his mere existence entails an "insurrection" against the nation and the revolutionary state (*R*, 66–71). This is the stuff of unrelieved ideological fanaticism.

In *Reflections on the Revolution in France*, Burke stated the real truth. At the end of the ancien régime, the French monarchy was "rather a despotism in appearance than in reality." And the famed English statesman and political philosopher added that the reign of Louis XVI should not be confused with "Persia bleeding under the ferocious sword of Thamas Kouli Khân." But that was precisely how Robespierre saw things, confusing the gentle and conscientious Louis XVI, a Christian of authentic conviction, with a brute and a beast. The king was transmogrified into a despot who must "die in order that the fatherland may live" (*R*, 67). In the name of absolute, inviolable, fanatical "principles" the king must die, so the people could live. There was a reason why Alexander Hamilton bristled when he heard the American Revolution compared to the French Revolution. The leaders of the latter—even some of its much-lauded moderate leaders—were in Hamilton's views "fanatics in political science," as he wrote in 1794. Bereft of the moderation that flows from prudence, Robespierre came to identify liberty with Virtue, and Virtue with Terror. That identification is literally deadly.

One of the strengths of Gauchet's book is the way it continually emphasizes the inability of Robespierre and his fellow fanatics to give serious thought to the art of governance in a political order at once popular and representative. Once Robespierre joined the Committee on Public Safety on July 27, 1793, his (and the revolution's) metamorphosis was complete. In place of governing, Robespierre and his allies searched for enemies, discerning corruption and conspiracy everywhere. Robespierre made clear that he preferred an "excess of patriotic fervor" over the "stagnation of moderatism" as he put it in a speech dated December 25, 1793 (*R*, 104). Moderation was the disposition of soul and civic stance that Robespierre loathed above all. His full embrace of fanaticism in the name of virtue and revolutionary principle reached a morally insane apex in his infamous speech of February 5, 1794. There, he announced that the revolution was endangered by "depraved men" who regarded it "as a trade and the Republic as a spoil" (*R*, 112–13). *L'Incorruptible* had declared war on everyone and everything in the name of an impossible purity.

He saw ill-defined collusion everywhere. "Virtue and Terror" was the only legitimate response to such corruption and such conspiracies. Camille Desmoulins had accused the Jacobins and the sansculottes, the Parisian revolutionary mob, of succumbing to out-and-out despotism. Robespierre did not dispute the point. But in a speech dated February 5, 1794,[2] he insisted that the "government of the Revolution is the despotism of liberty against tyranny," a distinction that was specious in these circumstances. Robespierre had once thought the death penalty an abomination. Now he confused justice—"prompt, severe, inflexible"—with Terror and loudly proclaimed Virtue without Terror to be weak and ineffectual (*RVT*, 115). Robespierre's fanatical defense of Terror in the name of the "Rights of Man" and Virtue properly understood is the quintessence of ideological despotism.

Robespierre was too fanatically dedicated to abstract principles to ever learn how "to govern the Revolution," in Gauchet's apt formulation (*R*, 88). Terror came to substitute for prudent and effective governance—an instrument that devoured its children, to use the memorable image from that time. Besides the guillotine and the pursuit of enemies in every corner of French society, Robespierre increasingly promoted, almost alone, a new "cult of the Supreme Being" (*R*, 49, 130–36, 148–54). He hated the Christian religion but worried that moral rot would follow the cruel and draconian de-Christianization campaigns. He worried that ordinary people would spend *décadi*—the tenth day of the week and the substitute for Sunday in the surreal revolutionary calendar—drinking in taverns (in this, he was not wrong) (*R*, 130). But most revolutionary leaders did not share Robespierre's obsession with his new cult. It floundered and with it Robespierre's political fortunes. The final straw came with the Law of 22 Prairial Year II (June 10, 1794), which established a legal obligation of all citizens to inform on everyone they suspected of counterrevolution, criminality, or subversion (*R*, 151). More blood began to flow and everyone (at least in principle) was obliged to be complicit in a regime of Terror. It was hard for even seasoned revolutionaries to see liberty at work in revolutionary government by denunciation and guillotine.

On the ninth of Thermidor Year II, *Le Tyran*, as Robespierre came to be called, was unmasked before the Convention. He and his supporters equivocated, in part because making incendiary speeches could not get them out of this bind (*R*, 164). In his own eyes, Robespierre died a martyr to the revolution. In the eyes of others, he was a tyrant and terrorist. But he was not a tyrant in the traditional sense. Instead, Robespierre was the revolutionary ideologue turned tyrant, the man who embodied the destructive fanaticism of principles that know no limits and are bereft of all prudence and moderation. Gauchet quotes a contemporary of Robespierre's, an obscure journalist named Cassat the Elder, who highlighted the ultimate paradox: "The fact remains that Robespierre exercised a very real tyranny and that he himself did not suspect that he was a tyrant" (*R*, 185). That is the hallmark of the ideological obfuscation of reality. Robespierre revealed the tyranny inherent in liberty and virtue when they lose sight of the moderation inherent in true principles.

In this estimable book, Marcel Gauchet might have put more emphasis on the evil that is ideological Manichæism, the temptation of ideologues and revolutionaries everywhere to localize evil and see its embodiment in suspect groups, whose elimination (or even "cancellation") will lead the world forward to revolutionary bliss. We witnessed this mechanism at work in the totalitarian regimes and ideologies of the twentieth century, the regimes that gave rise to death camps, gulags, and killing fields. We see the same impulse at work in the coercive virtue signaling that is the specialty of the woke. If they have their (unimpeded) way, why should we expect a happier or less tyrannical outcome? Are intellectual elites in the Western world capable of learning any salutary lessons from these misbegotten ideological adventures? Sadly, the record so far is not encouraging. We seem strangely impervious to the lessons of experience.

The New Jacobins

One of the most fashionable magazines on the American left today is called *Jacobin*. Is this revolutionary kitsch, reckless provocation, or just pure blindness? All of the above, I venture to guess. In 2017, the same year that he published a book lauding Lenin's theoretical and practical achievements, the leftist celebrity-intellectual Slavoj Žižek published a volume of Robespierre's speeches called *Virtue and Terror: Maximilien Robespierre*. The speeches themselves are useful for documentary purposes, as we have already shown. But Žižek's clever if truly deplorable introduction celebrates revolutionary terror as "Divine Violence" (*RVT*, vii–xxix) and mocks liberals and even leftists in France today who want to separate humanism from terror. With another well-known neo-Communist, the fashionable and ever more perverse French philosopher-ideologue Alain Badiou, Žižek denounces this as an unforgivable "political regression" (*RVT*, xiii). To be sure, Žižek takes an occasional swipe at the excesses of Stalinism, although he has no real ground for doing so. But he nonetheless insists that the "couple Virtue-Terror promoted by Robespierre" remains *the* key to human and political emancipation (*RVT*, xiii). The guillotine, anyone? Žižek defends what he calls the "abyss of the [revolutionary] act," wherever it may lead.

Is this posturing or a practical program? Once again, a bit of both, I suspect. As Roger Scruton ably put it in his treatment of Žižek (and Alain Badiou) in the 2015 edition of *Fools, Frauds, and Firebrands: Thinkers of the New Left*,

> *Žižek's defense of terror and violence, his call for a new party organized on Leninist principles, his celebration of Mao's Cultural Revolution, the thousands of deaths notwithstanding and indeed lauded as part of the meaning of a politics of Leftist action—all this might have served to discredit Žižek among more moderate left-wing readers, were it not for the fact that it is never possible to be sure that he is serious.*[3]

None of this excuses Žižek's utter lack of political responsibility and his "systematic" defense of the indefensible. I know from speaking on an untold number of college campuses that this clever but shameful apologist for revolutionary tyranny and terror, "Divine Violence," is *far* better known by the young than such anti-totalitarian titans as Aleksandr Solzhenitsyn, Czesław Miłosz, Václav Havel, and Leszek Kołakowski. As Saint Augustine wrote, *it is by our loves that we are finally defined.* This continuing indulgence toward revolutionary fanaticism ought to be a reason for deep concern, even alarm.

Sources and Suggested Readings

IN ADDITION to Marcel Gauchet's firm but judicious treatment of the fanaticism inherent in Robespierre's versions of popular sovereignty and the "Rights of Man," I recommend the reader turn to Francois Furet's *The French Revolution, 1770–1814* (Hoboken: John Wiley & Sons, 1996) for a vivid historical narrative that describes the dramatic unfolding of the French Revolution as well as the endless self-radicalization of its egalitarian ideological foundations.

FOR BURKE'S evocative account of the monarchy of the French ancien régime as "rather a despotism in appearance than in reality," see *Reflections on the Revolution in France,* ed. Frank Turner (New Haven: Yale University Press, 2003), 105–08.

SEE ROGER SCRUTON, *Fools, Frauds, and Firebrands: Thinkers of the New Left* (London: Bloomsbury, 2019), 261, for an excellent description of Žižek's self-conscious and all-too-clever oscillation between revolutionary fanaticism and postmodern irony.

CHAPTER 6

MARX AND MARXISM: EMANCIPATION AS SERVITUDE AND ESSENTIAL QUESTIONS FORECLOSED

LET US TURN from Robespierre to that great admirer of the Jacobins, Karl Marx. It is now over two hundred years since Karl Marx was born. As self-described socialists and even Communists gain attention, especially among the young, it is once again time for a reckoning on the Marxism of Marx. Marx famously spoke in 1848 of a specter haunting Europe—the "specter of Communism." All the powers in the world, he noted, had entered into a "holy alliance" to "exorcise"[1] the presence of Communism from the European and world stage (*MER*, 473). At the same time, Marx announced the death knell of the political and economic order he unilaterally called "capitalism." In the guise of a merely "scientific" analysis, he denounced this order for dehumanizing human beings and for leading to the comprehensive "pauperization" of the vast proletarian underbelly of modern industrial society (*MER*, 478–83). Today, we are more likely to pronounce the death of Marxism than of the liberal capitalist order that gave rise to Marx's fear and loathing.

Ingeniously combining pseudoscience and moral indignation, Marx limned a vision of a posthistorical and postpolitical order without contradictions or conflict, one that would achieve unprecedented prosperity and a new horizon marked by "human emancipation." This would be the realization and triumph of something Marx mysteriously called "species-being," an undifferentiated humanity and a society without conflict. A prophet of historical inevitability, Marx was also a committed "voluntarist" who welcomed revolutionary eruptions where they occurred and encouraged them along the way. His occasional preference for armed putsches against the "class enemy" is apparent in his enthusiasm for the French revolutionary commune of 1871. It is evident as well in his flirtation with the idea that Communist revolution could begin in Russia, even if the nation didn't meet all the official Marxist preconditions of industrial development necessary for socialist revolution (on this, see his and Engels's 1882 preface to the Russian edition of *The Communist Manifesto*).

Emancipating the World

Economist, prophet of capitalism's doom and an inevitable and blissful Communist future, and revolutionary agitator par excellence, Marx hated the world as it was. His goal was revolution—not merely political revolution or emancipation, but a wholesale change in the order of things: the aforementioned "human emancipation." For the German ideologist, there was no human nature or "natural order of things" that needed to be respected even as one worked to promote humane and salutary change. It is a mistake to apply categories such as "eternal justice" to Marx's political reflection, an identification that would have appalled the author of *The Communist Manifesto*. As he put it in 1845 in his "Theses on Feuerbach," the "philosophers have only *interpreted* the world, in various ways; the point however is to *change* it" (*MER*, 145). This comes from the young Marx, but it remained a profound sentiment of his until his death in 1883. Marx was not an advocate of reform, however radical. He did not work for "social justice" like a good humanitarian. Instead, he advocated something like metaphysical rebellion against the human condition. His humanism—and historicism—were distinctively inhumane, atheistic to the core, and entailed something like a gnostic revolt against reality. Eric Voegelin and Alain Besançon have demonstrated as much, and they have yet to be refuted convincingly.

For those looking for a humane alternative to the consumer society and to the excesses of "late capitalism," Marx does not in any way challenge the established view that the modern project ought to culminate in the thoroughgoing conquest of nature, to borrow a term from Descartes.

He praised capitalist globalization as its most noble and desirable feature and had no quarrel with a materialist cornucopia as the final goal of human existence (even if the young Marx—the one attractive to the New Left—sometimes prefers "being" to "having"). In his early years, Marx sometimes preferred "authenticity" to material prosperity. But that is not the conclusion of the mature Marx, the Marx who affected history and whose thought gave rise to Marxism-Leninism and all its derivations.

Rousseau, for all his other faults, provides a much more humane and convincing alternative to the pathologies of commercial society. His thought retained some real connections with the classical emphasis on self-restraint and the incompatibility of luxury with republican virtue. Moreover, Marx's thought cannot provide a philosophical grounding for calls for social equity and the promotion of a genuinely civic common good. Marx was not the first philosopher or political economist to speak of "class struggle." Aristotle, Madison, and Guizot knew of the phenomenon well before Marx. They, unlike Marx, tried to moderate—and calibrate—class struggle in the name of justice and the common good. These indispensable categories have *no* place whatsoever in the political economy or political philosophy of Marx. Marx thus cannot provide the intellectual foundations of a decent, moderate, or responsible Left in our democratic societies. To suggest otherwise is to engage in wishful thinking and the worst kind of philosophical and historical revisionism.

Some, such as the distinguished Catholic philosopher Alasdair MacIntyre, think Marx became relevant again—in fact, ever more relevant—after the fall of European Communism. On this account, the Marxism of Marx no longer has to carry the noose of Soviet Communism around its neck. The Soviet tragedy is thus consigned to the past, and questions about Marx's (partial) responsibility for the tragedies of the twentieth century can be safely ignored. Marx thus becomes a cipher or symbol for any and all reservations about capitalist modernity. This leads to absurdities in MacIntyre's own thought: Marx, the scourge of the "idiocy of village life," somehow justifies the conservative communitarianism to be found in isolated Icelandic and Irish fishing villages!

[71]

Marx, a thoroughgoing modernist and cosmopolitan, would be appalled by this, too!

Marx himself spoke of the necessary unity of theory and practice and promoted class struggle, violent revolution, and the leap from historical "necessity" to revolutionary "freedom" wherever he could. He did not promote the bloodless academic theory that Alain Badiou and Slavoj Žižek call "the idea of Communism," even as they write half-ironic encomiums to liberating terror under Lenin, Stalin, and Mao (they seem perversely obsessed with the "glories" of the Cultural Revolution, that Maoist descent into reckless murder, mayhem, and cultural destruction). As Roger Scruton has beautifully highlighted, Marxism has become the last refuge for assorted fools, frauds, and scoundrels, and apologists for totalitarianism in the academy. It is even a path for amateur intellectuals to find fortune and fame. As we have seen, it has allowed someone such as Žižek to become an intellectual celebrity defending, with a wink and a nod, "lost causes" of an egregiously ideological sort.

Unlike the neo-Communists, and to his credit, MacIntyre takes moral virtue seriously and thus refuses to justify the unjustifiable. His tendency to indulge Marx is consequently all the more mysterious, perhaps a residue of the antibourgeois ire that inspired him as a young Marxist theorist and activist. Antibourgeois ire inspires both the Stalinist activist and the communitarian romantic without relativizing or identifying the two stances. None of this is to suggest that we must rest content with a so-called market ideology that announces soulless globalization as our fate. Non-Marxists might learn to rediscover the *political* in political economy, even if in a distinctly non-Marxist way.

At the same time, MacIntyre's ahistorical appropriation of Marx evades the necessary task of assigning responsibility for the ravages of Marxism-Leninism in the twentieth century.

What Naturally Follows from Revolution

It will not do, as the admirable Polish philosopher Lezsek Kołakowski argued more than once, to accept the claim that Marx would have been appalled by the gulag archipelago, or Leninist-Stalinist-Maoist repression, or Stalin's so-called cult of personality.[2] That's probably true, even if Marx's powerful invective mocked "formal freedoms" and endorsed the "dictatorship of the proletariat" as a necessary step on the way toward that vagary he called "human emancipation" under which the state would somehow mysteriously "wither away" (*MER*, 490–91). The great French anti-Communist social and political thinker Raymond Aron was fascinated with the "Marxism of Marx" and thought that Marx was in certain moments an economist of real talent and "rich and subtle" insights.[3] But, as Aron argued in his 1983 *Memoirs*, it was Marx's transparently "false ideas" that left their terrible mark on the twentieth century: his doctrine of "surplus value" (with all profit denounced as thievery and exploitation) encouraged nationalization of even small businesses and trades as well as the illusion that one could eliminate markets and the "economic realm" altogether (see Lenin's "War Communism," which produced a deadly famine and a sustained assault on the independent peasantry in Russia). Both Aron and Kołakowski understood that the search for total unity, "species-being," led inexorably to unprecedented tyranny. Political liberty and the "formal" or "constitutional" freedoms had a dignity that Marx never began truly to appreciate. As Aron argued in the conclusion of his *Memoirs*, as an "economist-prophet" Marx was a "putative ancestor of Marxism-Leninism," and thus a "cursed sophist who holds his part of responsibility in the horrors of the twentieth century" (*M*, 468–69). This fact cannot be denied or ignored without turning a willfully blind eye to the darkest realities of the twentieth century.

In *The Soviet Tragedy*, the remarkable Russianist Martin Malia persuasively demonstrated the essential connection between the Marxism of Marx and the murderous totalitarian regimes of the twentieth century. "Maximalist socialism" of the Leninist-Stalinist variety finds powerful support in the "four abolitions" unapologetically put forward in the second part of *The Communist Manifesto*: the abolition of private property, the abolition of the traditional family, the abolition of religion, and the abolition of countries and nations (*MER*, 490–99). How does one abolish the moral contents of life without an unprecedented project of tyranny, terror, and centralization? And how does one expect a "revolutionary state," fully endorsed by Marx, to somehow "wither away"? In his "Letter to the Soviet Leaders," a work we have already drawn on (see chapter 3), Aleksandr Solzhenitsyn correctly diagnosed Marx with "sheer ignorance of human nature." Of course, Marx and Engels wryly suggested that bourgeois capitalism was already "abolishing" these traditional contents of human life and that Communism would simply consign them more quickly to the grave (*MER*, 483–89). But Malia's central point holds: Communism, from Petrograd to the South China Seas, entails an unremitting war on what Marx himself called the "material and spiritual elements of life." The post-Communist utopia is a chimera, deeply at odds with human nature, a vision of the future that is literally *unthinkable*. Leninism-Stalinism is the effectual truth of the Marxism of Marx *whether Marx intended it or not*. It is at a minimum one legitimate and even predictable outcome of the Marxist project. To what enduring and binding standards of justice could Marx appeal to condemn and resist Lenin's monstrous call (in his revealing January 1918 essay "How to Organize the Competition") for the triumphant Communist revolutionaries to "purge the Russian lands of all the harmful insects" such as "malingering" workers, recalcitrant peasants, independent intellectuals, merchants and men of commerce, religious believers, and political opposition from the Right and the Left?[4] As Solzhenitsyn noted in *The Gulag Archipelago*, Marx and Engels themselves taught that the "old bourgeois machinery of compulsion had to be broken up, and *a new one created* immediately in its place. As the great Russian writer sardonically added, "How in establishing the dictatorship of the proletariat, could they delay with a new type of prison" and a new kind of police? Lenin thus remained perfectly faithful to his Marxist inspiration.

Eric Voegelin called Marx an "intellectual swindler" in his polemical and provocative *Science, Politics, and Gnosticism*.[5] In that work, Voegelin accused Marx, with some justification, of refusing to allow certain questions to even be asked. What would Voegelin make of the passage in the second part of the *Manifesto* where Marx shamelessly declares that the "charges against Communism from a religious, a philosophical, and, generally, from an ideological standpoint, are not deserving of serious attention" (*MER*, 489)? Can we call such an unrelieved dogmatist a philosopher open to the truth of things? We have here a portent of the nationalization of the mind that would be the fate of human beings under "really existing" socialism. The essential human questions asked by religion and philosophy were banned by the ideocratic state, with the ready approval avant la lettre of Marx himself. Marx bears a heavy responsibility for the closure to the life of reason that marked every Communist society in the twentieth century. As we see, multiple roads lead from the Marxism of Marx to the tragedies of the twentieth century.

Questions Foreclosed

Can we still learn from Marx? Of course we can, despite everything. In a 1984 essay called "Totalitarianism and the Problem of Political Representation," the French political philosopher Pierre Manent, no Marxist of any stripe, shows how Marx's "On the Jewish Question" (1843) continues to illuminate the dynamics of a liberal order (we of course have nothing to learn from Marx's violent invective in that piece against Judaism as a form of "hucksterism").[6] As Manent shows, Marx brilliantly demonstrates the *diminutio capitis* that the "contents of life" undergo in a liberal society. The modern representative state exists to protect rights: as Manent paraphrases Marx, "in order for there to be religious freedom, there has to be religion, to have economic liberty," there must be private property and a market economy.

The liberal capitalist order thus *presupposes* property, family, religion, knowledge, and so forth. But it only fully *recognizes* individuals with their rights. A conservative or conservative liberal can draw from Marx a most un-Marxian conclusion: the goods of life must not be unduly eroded if the liberal order is to have meaningful contents of life that it can truly protect and represent. Of course, Marx's path is not that of liberal conservatism: he wants to replace the partial *political* emancipation

[75]

promoted by liberal capitalism with a wholly untenable and radically utopian *human* emancipation. Marx thus radicalizes and makes even more troubling the spiritual quandary of a liberal society. Marx continues to merit attentive reading leavened by alertness to the dogmatism, revolutionary impatience, and the quest for metaphysical rebellion that ultimately make his thought dangerous and untenable. But we do not want to imitate Marx in closing off these questions prematurely. Every student of politics and political philosophy must spend time with Marx, even if only to learn what to avoid.

Sources and Suggested Readings

FOR A MEASURED but not uncritical account of Alasdair MacIntyre's efforts to meld residues of Marxism with his own idiosyncratic Thomism, see Emile Perreau-Saussine, *Alasdair MacIntyre: An Intellectual Biography*, trans. Nathan Pinkoski (South Bend: University of Notre Dame Press, 2022).

MARTIN MALIA's *The Soviet Tragedy: A History of Socialism in Russia, 1917–1991* (New York: Free Press, 1994), also referenced in chapter 3, will remain for a long time to come the definitive account of ideology and utopia in power.

CHAPTER 7

DOSTOEVSKY ON THE SPIRIT OF REVOLUTIONARY NEGATION

Many ... greeted the twentieth as a century of elevated reason, in no way imagining the cannibalistic horrors that it would bring. Only Dostoevsky, it seems, foresaw the coming of totalitarianism.

—ALEKSANDR SOLZHENITSYN (1993)

THE RECENT 150TH anniversary of the publication of Dostoevsky's *Demons* (also known as *Devils* and perhaps less accurately as *The Possessed*) provided a welcome opportunity to reengage this timely and timeless literary dissection of moral and political nihilism. In it, Dostoevsky gathered all his imaginative and prophetic powers to confront the spirit of radical negation that defines the modern revolutionary project. This powerful novel is at once an unerringly accurate diagnosis of the sickness of soul that drives the totalitarian temptation as well as an inexhaustible literary monument to the ideological scourge that is coextensive with late modernity. It is at moments darkly humorous even as it delves into spiritual and political pathologies of the first order.

As Aleksandr Solzhenitsyn remarked about his great literary and spiritual forbear, Dostoevsky had an uncanny ability to see both profound truths about the soul and the human condition, and to foresee in all its demonic depths the totalitarian tragedy that would come to mark and deform the twentieth century. In *The Rebel*, another Nobel Laureate in literature, Albert Camus, turned to Dostoevsky to rescue himself from the moral abyss that haunted existentialism and to diagnose the totalitarian temptation in all its amplitude. As we in the United States confront new waves of moralistic fanaticism and toxic nihilism, as spiritual and cultural repudiation have become both fashionable and obligatory, and as many young people and pseudointellectuals bow before the cult of revolution and increasingly fashionable nostalgia for Communism, it is time to turn once again to Dostoevsky's jarring literary and political masterpiece as a source of spiritual nourishment and enduring wisdom.

In this essay, I will not be foolish or daring enough to try to summarize Dostoevsky's achievement in that work or to sketch the argument and action of *Demons* as a whole. Throughout I have drawn on the translation of *Demons* by Richard Pevear and Larissa Volokhonsky.[1] Instead, I will highlight some of its more evocative and instructive themes and passages to help us limn a path forward amidst our contemporary crisis. I will tentatively suggest that Dostoevsky's positive vision or alternative to regnant nihilism is perhaps less convincing or compelling than his unerring diagnosis of the demons that are revolutionary nihilism, political atheism, "half-science" or scientism, and an incipient totalitarianism that combines moral fanaticism with contempt for the primordial distinction between good and evil.

The Faces of Evil

If Dostoevsky successfully resists the demonic abstractions of the age, he never covers over the personal face of the evil that threatens the spiritual and political integrity of modern peoples. In that sense, his main characters are indeed concrete carriers of demonic evil. They are literally *possessed* by the spirit of negation or destruction that defines what Christ in the Gospel of John calls the "Father of Lies" (John 8:11). The brilliant, handsome, and charismatic Stavrogin, né Nikolai Vsevolodovich Stavrogin, embodies gifts gone terribly awry, a natural aristocrat (of sorts) who inexorably leads everyone astray. Confused by his simple wife (whom he married on a mischievous lark) for a prince and by the secret revolutionary circle (to which he is tied without exactly being a member) for the consummate revolutionary leader, his ability to lead his followers is marked only by the preternatural ability to corrupt them. His alluring charisma draws people in even as he does not hesitate to manipulate and sully souls. Beyond his superficially aristocratic countenance, he is decisively "beyond good and evil."

Stavrogin's arrival in a fictional Russian provincial town ultimately unleashes evil pure and simple. He has raped and killed because his soul craves perverse pleasure, an ironic indifference to good and evil, and ultimately a form of self-deification that is inseparable from self-destruction. He halfheartedly and ultimately insincerely attempts a confession, but the holy retired Bishop Tikhon, who lives in the same town, sees through his depraved manipulations. Stavrogin wishes to be free of all "prejudices," including the one that leads a decent soul to prefer good to evil. As Bishop Tikhon discerns, Stavrogin's is a "mortally wounded heart" (D, 706). Along the way, the faux aristocrat does nothing to discourage the engineer Kirillov from choosing the path of suicide as a means of self-deification through the triumph of "self-will." In shooting himself, in escaping fear and pain, but also the benevolent sovereignty of God, Kirillov believes he will become a "man-God" through the act of pure, willful negation (D, 115). His is another path to Stavrogin's deadly goal of sustained revolt against the order of creation.

In different ways, Stavrogin and Kirillov both choose to become Autonomous Men in a truly demonic manner. This decision can only lead to murder, spiritual madness, and, finally, suicide. Their paths are less directly political than the circle of revolutionary nihilists depicted in *Demons*. But in a certain sense they are even more demonic since they aim less at an earthly paradise—however misbegotten—than becoming gods, or antigods, themselves. With both, self-affirmation is inseparable from nihilistic self-destruction, from spiritual and physical suicide.

Political Nihilism and Egalitarian Despotism

The tiny circle of revolutionary nihilists in *Demons* are modelled on the real-life cell that existed in Saint Petersburg around Sergei Nechaev. This conspiratorial circle preached the gospel of revolutionary destruction and in 1869 murdered an apostate from their movement, Ivan Ivanov, who had distanced himself from their revolutionary psychosis. This world too is "beyond good and evil" and quite emphatically so. The leader of the madcap circle in Dostoevsky's novel, at once demonic and absurd, is the purely malicious Pyotr Stepanovich Verkhovensky. He leads the lost and willful souls in his nihilist revolutionary circle to believe that they are one of an untold number of such circles prepared to unleash revolutionary destruction in Russia as a whole. He is a master manipulator of his revolutionary underlings who sense his contempt for them even as they act as his obedient foot soldiers. When the action begins in *Demons*, the younger Verkhovensky has only recently returned to town. But his destructive presence is immediately felt by all. He plots murder and mayhem with singular determination. He privately admits that he is a "crook" as well as a "socialist," although the two avocations are by no means in contradiction in his mind or that of others (*D*, 420).

Within days, he has become the manipulative intimate of Yulia von Lembke, the wife of the liberal governor of the province. She is not alone among educated society in coddling and admiring the "progressive little notions," as Dostoevsky once called them, that her peers heard and saw on display from the nihilists. Dostoevsky chronicles the pathetic, slavish deference of liberal society toward incipient totalitarianism with dark and biting humor. The governor, Andrei Antonovich von Lembke, only sees the revolutionaries for the heartless and destructive nihilists that they are after they unleash murder, arson, and mayhem at Yulia von Lembke's literary soirée put on to help local governesses. He ludicrously compares himself to a "Tory" who will stabilize and restrain the untried and unhinged ideas of the revolutionary "Whigs" (*D*, 314). This analogy is so preposterous that it is hard to believe that anyone in a position of political responsibility could believe it in the first place. The "Tories" Governor von Lembke refers to are indulgent progressives and no liberals at all. And the "Whigs" in the story are nihilistic revolutionaries and hardly defenders of true human freedom. The analogy is strained—and in the end utterly illusory.

Fathers and Sons

Pyotr Stepanovich Verkhovensky did not emerge out of thin air. He is the son of Stepan Verkhovensky, a liberal-progressive intellectual of another era. A protégé of Varvara Stavrogina, an aristocratic and onetime owner of "souls" (serfs) who prides herself on her openness to fashionable ideas and to the life of culture more generally, she wants a house intellectual around to keep her informed and cultivated (and sufficiently, but only sufficiently, progressive to boot). Her relationship with Verkhovensky père is at once strained, affectionate, authoritarian, and high-strung. Varvara dotes on her son Nikolai, but senses deep down that something is terribly wrong. The liberal idealist Stepan Verkhovensky neglects both his son (whom he sent away to various aunts to tutor and raise) and the educated Stavrogin himself rather haphazardly and to disastrous effect.

Stepan Trofimovich Verkhovensky is intellectually incoherent and less than fully aware that he has been playing with fire. He fights terribly with his son Pyotr Stepanovich, whose destructive ideas and ferocious temperament truly frighten him. In one scene in chapter 4 ("All in Expectation") the two "discuss" Nikolai Chernyshevsky's extremist revolutionary tract *What is to be Done?*, whose title and destructive revolutionary nihilism would be freely adopted by Lenin himself. Stepan studies the novel to see where this strange destructiveness had its roots. He wants to know—and rebut—their revolutionary "catechism." But Stepan begins by making a fatal concession: "I agree that the author's basic idea is correct," and quickly adds "but so much more horrible for that!" (*D*, 303–04).

By affirming the revolutionary ideal that animates this turgid and nihilistic catechism, Stepan has left himself vulnerable to the more willful and consistent affirmations of his son. Verkhovensky père wants to be "progressive" without drawing all the revolutionary and nihilistic conclusions inherent in his position. But starting with the first premises of revolutionary ideology, it is hard to cogently argue that the doctrine has been "perverted, distorted, mutilated!" as Stepan does (*D*, 304). Pyotr Stepanovich can readily mock his father for his incoherent mixture of decency and progressive ideology. Pyotr is thus the faithful heir of *What is to be Done?*, as Lenin would be a generation or two later. Verkhovensky fils knows that his father cannot have it both ways. In that exchange, the

Russian generational conflict between liberal, progressive fathers and nihilistic sons is brilliantly encapsulated.

Stepan Trofimovich ultimately redeems himself in a "conversion" that, while not straining credulity, is less than completely believable. At Yulia Mikhailovna von Lembke's ball, Stepan proclaims his fidelity to beauty and argues that Shakespeare and Raphael are more important than any revolution—or even the freeing of the serfs. They represent a "beauty" that is above all sociopolitical concerns (D, 485–86). After the revolutionary conflagration, a sickly Stepan Trofimovich, consumed by fever, asks for the account of the Gadarene swine (Luke 8: 32–36)—which serves as an epigraph to the book as a whole—to be read to him. He now immediately appreciates the demons of that famous scriptural passage for who they are. He commits himself to fighting the "big and little demons" that have "accumulated in our great and dear sick man," the Russia that he has always loved (characteristically affirmed in French, the language of educated society and intellectual pretense). Delirious and on the verge of losing consciousness, Stepan dedicates himself to preaching the Gospel and to loving poor, sick Russia. Compared to his son, he was only partially possessed all along. But his demons, "insane and raging," have now gone over the cliff, too (for all these quotations, see D, 654–55). His conversion is a sign of hope and perhaps foreshadows a promising restoration of political and spiritual sanity.

At the heart of Demons is the revolutionary program of the nihilists themselves. Here Dostoevsky discerned where revolution leads with unerring accuracy. Pyotr Stepanovich champions the revolutionary program of Shigalyov, a revolutionary theorist possessed by ideology of the most fanatical kind, and down to the smallest details. Shigalyov, the younger Verkhovensky, almost madly proclaims, "invented equality!" The new egalitarian despotism, "paradise on earth," will self-consciously create "equality in slavery." True freedom, Shigalyov insists, can only be found in "perfect despotism" (for all these quotations, see D, 417). Everything must be leveled since high aspiration, spiritual or intellectual, gives rise to dreaded inequalities. Human greatness, high and noble aspiration, must be crushed and beaten out of the human soul. Slaves, we are told, need rulers, and egalitarianism demands despotism of an unprecedented variety.

This demonism knows no limits: Since higher abilities cannot be tolerated but instead must be warred on, nobility must be "banished or executed" (D, 417). In this paradise-turned-nightmare, "Cicero's tongue is cut off, Copernicus's eyes put out, Shakespeare is stoned—this is Shigalyism!" (D, 417). Pyotr Stepanovich, following Shigalyov, un-abashedly declares that there can be no freedom or equality without a truly inhuman and unprecedented kind of despotism. With unerring accuracy, the younger Verkhovensky tells us that one hundred million people will perish at the hands of egalitarian and socialist despotism (D, 405–06), the exact number of the victims of Communism in the twentieth century chronicled by 1998's *The Black Book of Communism*. The great Dostoevsky could truly *see…*

The Party of Nihilism

In this same remarkably revelatory chapter (chapter 8, "Ivan the Tsarevich"), Pyotr Stepanovich Verkhovensky chronicles all the "soft uto-pians" (the phrase is Reinhold Niebuhr's) who have already succumbed to moral nihilism and political insanity: children who have been taught by their teachers to laugh at God, lawyers who shamelessly defend the deeds of murderers for fear of being insufficiently progressive, school-boys who kill "just to see how it feels," academics who defend murder as either a sign of insanity or material necessity, but never of evil. They are "ours," he proclaims, fellow travelers and even unbeknownst foot soldiers of the party of nihilism. Many are "drunk" with ideology; many more will "get themselves even drunker" (for all these quotations, see D, 420) inebriated by the cult of revolution, "half-science," angry atheism, and contempt for all permanent standards and solid foundations for the indispensable distinction between good and evil.

Dostoevsky's book speaks not only to the crisis enveloping Russia (one tied to, and initiated by, an intelligentsia that hates God, morality,

[83]

country, and simple decency), but also to the spiritual and political crisis that is coextensive with late modernity itself. *Demons* is a book for East and West alike, one for all those who wish to rescue the soul of modern man. With the descent into open nihilism comes the paradoxical possibility of spiritual and political resistance to these demons who have taken monstrous human form.

Dostoevsky is thus our master diagnostician of the entire soul-destroying project to replace God and the nation with all-consuming "self-will" and the nihilistic and eternally self-negating effort to turn Man into God. Yet, as in all his master works, the representatives of the forces of evil at times seem more powerful, evocative, and memorable than the forces of truth and goodness. A cursory comparison in *The Brothers Karamazov* of Ivan Karamazov to his brother Alyosha or even to Father Zossima supports this point. Alyosha and Zossima seem less substantial, and perhaps too meek or otherworldly, to truly take on the forces of demonic destruction. And the Christ of "The Legend of the Grand Inquisitor" says not a word but only gives the ominous Grand Inquisitor a kiss of peace—a powerful gesture, but one accompanied by passivity and extreme otherworldliness.

Of course, as Alain Besançon has noted, the writings of Dostoevsky have led many to convert to Christianity. Figures such as Konstantin Mochulsky, Romano Guardini, René Girard—and I would add Nikolai Berdyaev and Henri de Lubac—have found in Dostoevsky a voice of compelling Christian faith. Yet, in Dostoevsky's works, the negation of atheism and all its works seems to this reader more powerful, more compelling (at least rhetorically), than the positive affirmation of the Christian alternative. This is not to deny the reality and efficaciousness of Dostoevsky's faith, which is as much national as it is authentically religious in character.

Dostoevsky and Shatov

One character who seems to speak for Dostoevsky in *Demons* is Ivan Pavlovich Shatov, the son of Varvara Stavrogina's deceased valet, and a man of character and conviction who has freed himself from the grip of Stavrogin and the nihilistic circle around Pyotr Stepanovich Verkhovensky. As Jacob Howland has argued, he is one of the two characters in the book who genuinely converts, who switches from belief in a false god to genuine faith and is ultimately "spiritually healed." Near the end of the novel, before he is murdered by the revolutionaries who rightly fear he will turn them in to the authorities, Shatov commits himself to "preaching" God and proclaims the necessity of repentance rooted in shared guilt, the sinfulness that belongs to man as man (D, 579, 592–94). Shatov is an admirable character and largely a voice of truth. But, at the same time, his ambiguities largely reflect Dostoevsky's own. His Slavophilism, admirable and insightful in important respects, is questionably and incompletely Christian, for reasons I hope to illuminate.

In a forceful and memorable exchange with Stavrogin in chapter 1 of part II, "Night," Shatov challenges Stavrogin's demonic indifference to the distinction between good and evil and uses many of his words against him. He exposes the atheistic essence of socialism and the intimate connection between the nation and the affirmation of God (D, 250–54). So far, so good. "Seeking for God," he suggests, is at the heart of every great nation, culture, and people. Shatov powerfully exposes the despotism inherent in "half-science," a rationalism and scientism that cannot distinguish good and evil. Once again Shatov is absolutely on the mark. But more troublingly, he defends the particularity not only of a people's culture but of "its God." And he unequivocally states that "every nation has its own idea of evil and good" (D, 250–51). Here he goes badly astray.

This affirmation completely undercuts the universalism inherent in Orthodox faith and any cogent affirmation of natural justice against radical or thoroughgoing cultural and moral relativism. Stavrogin thus sees an opportunity and suggests that Shatov has "reduc[ed] God to a mere attribute of nationality." Shatov denies this, saying that he wants to "raise the nation up to God" (D, 250–51). Shatov, like Dostoevsky at certain moments at least, seems to identify Russian Christianity with what Solzhenitsyn has called "messianic national exclusiveness," which is at best a heresy and at worst a beguiling confusion and temptation. At the end of this exchange, Shatov affirms, "I believe in Russia, I believe in her Orthodoxy... I believe in the body of Christ... I believe that the new coming will take place in Russia ... I believe ..." But when Stavrogin interrupts to ask Shatov if he believes in God the latter affirms "I... I will believe in God" (D, 253). Shatov's faith is thus a work in progress, as much a political faith as religious faith, as I have already suggested.

As we have already noted, Shatov's religious conversion is more complete later in the novel right before he is cruelly murdered. Perhaps Richard Pevear and René Girard are right when they suggest that Dostoevsky sees and finally resists a certain temptation in Shatov's original position, one that identifies Christianity too much with the "Russian God" and the "Russian Christ." There is undoubtedly much Dostoevsky in Shatov and much Shatov in Dostoevsky, too. But I concur with Girard that the glorious author of Demons and The Brothers Karamazov cannot be summarily reduced to Slavophile ideology. The literary Dostoevsky, the spiritual Dostoevsky, is never a counterideologist. His soul, his insights, his commitment to transcendent truth can never be encapsulated within the narrow confines of a socio-political or national project, however choice-worthy or partially true.

In any case, the Slavophile aspects of Dostoevsky's thought and writings, his finding the mark of Christ in simple Russian people, and not spiritually desiccated intellectuals, is most beautifully articulated in his 1876 entry in The Writer's Diary on "The Peasant Marei,"[2] his father's serf who comforted the young Dostoevsky when he believed he was endangered by a wolf. Marei's natural and Christian tenderness, his unforced kindness, came to Dostoevsky as a revelation when he recalled it as an adult. In the benevolence of this "bestially ignorant serf" he saw the mark of Christ and a sign of the "advanced" spiritual "development of our Russian people" (DC, 464). And in the famous "Pushkin Speech," delivered in Moscow in 1880, Dostoevsky more successfully (and even sublimely) brought together his sense of the "mission of Russia" with "pan-European and universal" spiritual ideals rooted in the "general harmony," the brotherly harmony and accord promoted by Christ's Gospel (*DC*, 478–79). This harmony had nothing to do with the extinction of national distinctions that were for the Russian writer part of God's providential design. The Christian affirmation of Dostoevsky is at once radically particularistic and profusely universalistic. Therein, I suspect, lies the source of both its luminous strengths and its seductive temptations.

In conclusion, any engagement with Dostoevsky's greatest works, including *Demons*, must be a personal engagement as well as a spiritual, political, and literary one. The diagnostic genius of this master work is self-evident, and its ability to bring us back from the brink of nihilistic destruction is apparent to those with eyes to see. My hope is that others will be led to engage with a book that offers so much light for us to see our way amid the cultural, spiritual, and political darkness of our time. Let us be thankful for the gift to East and West alike that is the art and wisdom and spiritual insight of Fyodor Dostoevsky.

Sources and Suggested Readings

THE OPENING EPIGRAPH is drawn from Aleksandr Solzhenitsyn's 1993 address, "We have ceased to see the Purpose" in *The Solzhenitsyn Reader: New and Essential Writings, 1947–2005*, eds. Daniel J. Mahoney and Edward E. Ericson Jr. (Washington, DC: ISI, 2006), 598.

ALBERT CAMUS may have remained a nonbeliever, but his adamant rejection of revolutionary messianism and nihilism is profoundly indebted to Dostoevsky. See Camus, *The Rebel: An Essay on Man in Revolt*, trans. Anthony Bower (New York: Vintage, 1992).

FOR THE DRAMATIC HISTORICAL events that inspired the writing of *Demons*, see Richard Pevear's foreword to *Demons* (New York: Vintage, 1994), especially vii–xii. And for the differences and affinities between Dostoevsky and Shatov, see xvii–xviii.

FOR A PARTICULARLY CHALLENGING account of the doubts and ambiguities that continued to inform Dostoevsky's affirmation of Christian faith, see Alain Besançon, *The Falsification of the Good: Soloviev and Orwell*, trans. Matthew Screech (England: Claridge Press, 1994).

I AM INDEBTED to Jacob Howland, " 'Demons' at 150," *The New Criterion*, vol. 39, no. 7 (March 2021) for its helpful (and hopeful) account of Shatov's moral and intellectual development.

CHAPTER 8

THE LOST PROMISE OF 1989

THE YEAR 1989 proved to be the negation of 1793, if not 1789: an opportunity to free the Western mind from the ideological and totalitarian temptation. It is difficult for those of us who lived through a good part of the Cold War, when Communist hegemony over half of Europe (and many other places in the world) seemed more or less permanent, to fully appreciate that thirty-five years have passed since the annus mirabilis that was 1989. It was in that golden year that the peoples of East-Central Europe freed themselves from Communist bondage and began to reassert themselves as proud and independent nations. Communism was teetering in the Soviet Union, too, with Russians discovering that they were ill-served by an ideological regime that put foreign adventures—and utopian abstractions—above the well-being of the nation.

Poland was the first to go: The "roundtable" agreements peacefully turned over the governance of the country to a political opposition inspired by the Polish pope and the struggles of the underground *Solidarność* movement. Next, the Hungarians reburied Premier Imre Nagy in June of 1989, one of the heroes of the great anti-totalitarian revolution of 1956, and hundreds of thousands of people demanded political freedom and authentic nationhood. Even the relatively soft goulash Communism of János Kádár was finished. East Germans began fleeing their prison-state in the summer and fall of 1989, making their way to Hungary and then Austria and West Germany. Massive demonstrations followed in Leipzig and other major cities. Soon the repulsive Erich Honecker, the last of the East German hardliners, was summarily dismissed by the East German politburo.

The regime of the *Stasi* was paralyzed when confronted by a civil society demanding liberation from enforced lies. The Berlin Wall was breached on November 9, 1989, after a mid-level East German official inadvertently declared it open. By June of 1990, Germany was whole

[89]

and free. Soviet leader Mikhail Gorbachev may have had false hopes in a "Leninism with a human face," but his refusal to crush the revolutions of 1989 was surely a force for the good, and a precondition for everything that followed. And "perestroika" unintentionally took aim at the Ideological Lie: in 1987 Orwell was published in the Soviet Union, followed by Koestler in 1988, and then the unthinkable, excerpts from Solzhenitsyn's *Gulag Archipelago* in the fall of 1989 and in 1990. The end was surely near.

A passive and demoralized Czech people found their civic spirit and appeared en masse in the streets of Prague in 1988 and particularly in the fall of 1989. The dramatist, dissident, and repeated prisoner of the Communist regime Václav Havel orchestrated a peaceful revolution from his "base" in the Magic Lantern theater in Prague. And the impossible happened on January 1, 1990, when Havel was sworn in as the president of a free Czechoslovakian state, promising not to lie, as previous governments had lied, to the Czech and Slovak peoples. In Albania, Bulgaria, and Romania, the old guard remained in power while declaring themselves anti-Communists and patriots, declarations that were difficult to take at face value.

Still, by the beginning of 1990, Communism had clearly lost its legitimacy and could no longer serve as a plausible basis of political or national life anywhere in the east of Europe. It unequivocally stood for violence, mendacity, shortages, corruption, and national humiliation. I will go further: the events of 1989 were the end of a two-hundred-year cycle of "total revolution" inaugurated by the French Revolution and "perfected" by Bolshevism and its offspring (e.g. Maoism, Castroism, Pol Potism) in the twentieth century. The revolution of 1989 was a decisive repudiation of the ideological poisons that had deformed modernity. It is a decisive repudiation that many on the militant left would like to erase. There is absolutely no reason today for socialism—and even Communism—to have the prestige it has with many young Americans. Crucial lessons about the twentieth century have sadly not been passed on to young people in any serious or significant way. A crucial opportunity has been lost. We are paying the price in the emergence of a punishing woke despotism and new form of ideological Manichæism that rivals Jacobinism and Bolshevism in their efforts to morally annihilate "enemies of the people." Let us pray that physical annihilation doesn't follow down the line.

The Ideological Lie had been exposed as the chimera it has always been. The peoples behind the Iron Curtain cried out for a "normal" existence, freed from violence, lawlessness, and systematic mendacity. Their economic motives and concerns were real, in the order of things, but secondary. People can tolerate poverty, at least to some extent, but not the spiritual poverty of a regime built on force and deception. The soul inevitably revolts against efforts to suffocate it. The world was witnessing a new kind of revolution, one that vindicated human nature and the traditional moral contents of life, one that freely and proudly spoke the language of good and evil and truth and falsehood that has long been discredited in elite intellectual circles in the Western world. The spirit of 1989 was far from the soft nihilism of fashionable and always "ironic" postmodernism, which "deconstructed" all the old verities that resurfaced during the revolution of 1989. When Havel, Lech Wałęsa, Pope John Paul II, and Solzhenitsyn evoked the imperative of truth against the Ideological Lie, they were by no means being "ironic" or even "mystical" or "poetic." They evoked the soul as an *empirical* reality of the first order and saw their own struggles as a victory of reality over the deadly fictions that had been so tyrannically imposed on the Soviet peoples since 1917 and the people of East-Central Europe since 1945.

Impoverished Responses

But sophistic renderings of the news of 1989 reared their heads almost immediately. When well-known philosopher and man of letters Richard Rorty reviewed two volumes of the writings of the great Czech phenomenologist and philosopher Jan Patočka (a founding spokesman for Charter 77 who died under Security Service interrogation in 1977) in the *New Republic* in 1991, he expressed some embarrassment that Patočka and

Havel had seemed to really mean it when they appealed to the permanent imperative of "living in truth." Rorty clearly admired the two men but regretted that they were so naïve to believe that good and evil, truth and falsehood, have roots in the very structure of reality and the permanent nature and needs of the human soul. Two incommensurable worlds met, and Rorty revealed once more the shallowness of his mind and soul. For him—everything, life, death, language, love, truth, and falsehood—were contingent all the way down. He inhabited a world of linguistic constructions and "deconstructions"—and hence one of linguistic tyranny.

Rorty, a humane man in many ways, was not alone. In his famous essay "The End of History?,"[1] published in *The National Interest* in 1989, Francis Fukuyama, then an obscure analyst for the Rand Corporation, interpreted 1989 in a dramatically Hegelio-Marxist, and thus reductive, way. 1989 was not a salutary and liberating return of the "Real," of human nature in all its grandeur and misery, but the final moment in the ideological human drama. "History" itself was over, and with the defeat of European Communism, human beings had arrived, at least in principle, at the "end point of mankind's ideological evolution and the universalization of Western liberal democracy as the final form of government." There was, of course, some cleaning up that needed to be done. Pockets of nationalist passion and religious belief would persist, at least for a while, until the time they were domesticated by private life and shorn of all real genuine seriousness. But the "universal homogenous state" announced by Alexandre Kojève, the Russian-born Hegelio-Marxist philosopher and European Union bureaucrat (and some-time Soviet spy), had indeed arrived in principle. It had "found real-life embodiment" in the countries of postwar Western Europe, which Fukuyama freely admitted were "flabby, prosperous, self-satisfied, inward looking" and "weak-willed states," to boot.

A decade or so before, the French political thinker Raymond Aron had called the rump of free Europe "decadent"[2] and wondered if it had the civic and martial virtues to weather the challenges of the future. Aron had concluded that West Europeans saw themselves as the avant-garde of humanity, decisively leaving behind History, "whose letters are written in blood." But Aron was quite sure that there was no "end of History" and that the depoliticization of Western Europe was more of a pathology than a virtue. Aron died in November of 1983, but surely he would have seen in the revolution of 1989 a liberating moment that appealed to love of liberty and truth in their deepest manifestations.

In that sense, the men of 1989 were a challenge to a West that mistakenly—and superficially—thought history had come to an end. One mark of the intellectual poverty of Kojève's and Fukuyama's approach is that the denizens of the end of History could see the "universal homogenous state" embodied at various times in Bonapartist despotism (the World-Spirit on a horse, as Hegel described him at the Battle of Jena in 1806), in the full-scale murderous totalitarianism of Stalin's quasi-personalized Bolshevism, and in the soft, economistic, postpolitical European Community of the 1950s and 1960s. There is simply too much flexibility here, since the end of History can accommodate both the victory of liberal democracy and the murderous ravages of Communist totalitarianism. It is hard to be convinced by these philosophical acrobatics.

Why this contempt for the human spirit, for the view that the cardinal virtues—courage, justice, prudence, and temperance—will always speak to the human soul and be a permanent requirement of individual and collective life? Why this seeming complacency about the human spirit—and all the virtues—becoming obsolete? Of course, Fukuyama conceded that the end of History would make some, such as himself, sad. And in the book version of his article, *The End of History and the Last Man* (1992), he went further in suggesting that "boredom," and the absence of a viable field for spiritedness and high human endeavor, might reignite History after all. But it is fair to say that Fukuyama got the revolution of 1989 wrong, woefully wrong, by interpreting it in light of an inhuman and undesirable "universal homogenous state." Such an inverted perspective—judging the high from the perspective of the low—is a crucial barrier to moral and political understanding, as Leo Strauss once suggested.

The Resurgence of the Real

Those who showed most clarity about the Ideological Lie knew that political, religious, and national freedom could not be attained by a revolution in the conventional sense of the term. The Lie needed to be challenged, openly, truthfully, in the spirit of the indomitable Saint George slaying the dragons of old. Pope John Paul II did this when he evoked eternal and temporal truths that were denied by the ideological regime and were so central to the restoration of political, intellectual, religious, and national freedom. In 1983, speaking to young Poles at the sacred site of Jasna Gora, he beckoned them to reject fear, and "to be a person of conscience."[3] No Rortyan moral relativism or Kojèvian historicism there.

The Poles, the pope insisted, must learn once again to call good and evil by their names and to never confuse one for the other. They must have the courage to recover the "common inheritance whose name is Poland." Here, and in his great 1993 book *Memory and Identity*, Pope John Paul II spoke as a proud and principled Polish patriot, one who recognized the nation as a "natural human association." He knew that a patriotism worthy of the name would have a significant "historical price." Poles are not "so easily free": they must fight for it over and over again if need be. This was their fate, and their great privilege. This is far from the spirit of Kojève's last man at the end of History, content with personal enjoyments and a posthistorical descent into hedonism, softness, and self-indulgence. Pope John Paul II called on Poles to be neither hard (aggressive and cruel) nor soft (passive and morally indifferent). Instead, he called on them to be both Christians and patriots (a call, truth be told, unthinkable under this "Franciscan" pontificate).

Moreover, in a manner that reminds one of Solzhenitsyn's own "warnings to the West" in the 1970s, Pope John Paul II called on Poles and East Europeans more generally not to slavishly follow the materialism and soft relativism that was too often confused with liberty by many in the Western world. He hoped that the people of Eastern Europe had undergone such a "process of spiritual maturation" that they could still see, and vigorously affirm, "that God is the supreme guarantor of depends on an end to the conflict in Ukraine and a gradual less[...] animosity between Russia and the Western democracies.

For its part, East-Central Europe faces a *kulturkampf* of great [sign]icance. The old apparatchiks oppose a truthful confrontation with [...] ideological past and benefit from corruption because they, above [...] know how things work, or used to work. The genuine dissidents are co[n]tent that totalitarianism is a thing of the past but wonder how the high moral aspirations at the heart of 1989's great anti-totalitarian revolution have been forgotten so quickly. The more traditional among them fear that Ireland is their future, where gay marriage is celebrated and imposed on dissenting persons and groups, where Catholic nurses and doctors are required to perform abortions, and where Christianity is mocked by nearly the entire political and intellectual class. These were surely not the aspirations of *Solidarność* and the freedom-loving Polish pope.

It is hard to quarrel with Ryszard Legutko's claim in *The Demon in Democracy* that "liberal democracy" no longer means what it used to mean only two or three decades ago. It is openly relativistic and aggressively hostile to robust affirmations of the Good. Universities increasingly have no place for conservatives, traditional Jews, orthodox Christians, or other defenders of age-old marriage rooted in the natural complementarity of men and women. With the aggressive linguistic tyranny of gender theory and its 173 categories (and counting), human nature is denied in any recognizable, commonsense understanding of the term.

A new ideological "wooden language" is increasingly imposed on all. It might not be too early to call it a creeping totalitarianism. Legutko speaks boldly but with no real hyperbole when he writes: "Both sides," Communists and our newly radicalized defenders of postmodern liberal democracy, "share their dislike, sometimes bordering on hatred, *toward the same enemies*, the Church and religion, the nation, classical metaphysics, moral conservatism, and the family."[6] In the midst of the "dictatorship of relativism" emerging around us, a rearguard action, largely defensive in orientation, appears required to prevent the worst. But when the Law and Justice Party in Poland opposes LGBT ideology, they

human dignity and human rights." In doing so, they would surely reject "anthropocentric humanism," or "anthropocentricity," as Solzhenitsyn called it, and reaffirm the spiritual and moral foundations of democracy, rightly understood. This would demand civic courage and the ability to distinguish "liberty under God and the laws," as Tocqueville once eloquently called it, from "negative cultural models, so widespread in the West," that confuse the moral term liberty with a life of untrammeled autonomy and a reckless, groundless relativism.

Havel expressed similar thoughts, although in a somewhat more secular and even New Age idiom. Against the sophists, calculators, and economists whom Edmund Burke lamented in his *Reflections on the Revolution in France*, the Czech statesman declared in 1992's *Summer Meditations* that "Communism was overthrown by life, by thought, by human dignity."[4] He believed and repeated this endlessly in all his dissident and presidential writings: genuine politics is unthinkable without a responsibility rooted in what he called the "Memory of Being," a transcendental ground for genuine conscience and genuine responsibility.

Like Pope John Paul II, and yes, even like Solzhenitsyn, Havel (falsely perceived by some as a man of the Left) supported the full range of public and private liberties that inform a rule-of-law society. He placed constant stress on "moral deliberation and moral judgment," and he thought relativism, thoughtless scientism, and reductionism ate away at "spirit," "feeling," and "conscience," the crucial prerequisites of human dignity and a free and decent society. He was more of a cosmopolitan (and less of a partisan of the nation) than Solzhenitsyn or Pope John Paul II. But he, too, feared that "Europe" in its dominant, technocratic form, corroded self-government and the things of the spirit. Europe, he once commented, could not be reduced to the regulation of carrots.

Leaving Utopia Behind?

For all their differences, and they were often significant, it might be said that Solzhenitsyn, Pope John Paul II, and Havel all were tempted by a (very qualified) "utopia" of their own. They dreamed of a new kind of society, where freedom was accompanied by "repentance and self-limitation" (*TSR*, 527); where the Catholic spirit informed a democracy that valued persons as persons (Pope John Paul II); and defended an understanding of free politics rooted in moral judgment and a civility that went much deeper than good manners (Havel). Solzhenitsyn knew that evil could never be expunged from the soul and the world and fully appreciated that all ideological revolutions (which he also called "bloody, physical ones") only lead to tyranny, coercion, unprecedented mendacity, and a cruelty and fanaticism that ignored the inescapable drama of good and evil in the human soul.

But also Solzhenitsyn hoped that democratic man might learn to pay more attention to his soul and overcome, at least in part, the "excessive engrossment in everyday life" in modern, democratic societies that he lamented in his Harvard Commencement Address of 1978.[5] Havel speaks for all of our heroes when he wrote in his chapter "Politics, Morality, and Civility" from 1992's *Summer Meditations* that a conception of liberty and human dignity that addresses the needs of the soul should not be confused with the naïve hope that the internal struggle in each human soul between good and evil may one day come to an end. There will never be a heaven on earth, Havel insisted: such projects, always ideological in character, have been forever shattered and exposed by the evil, utopian enterprises of the twentieth century: "The world has had the worst experiences with utopian thinkers who promised all that." And as Solzhenitsyn wrote in 1993, fraternity can never be imposed politically, and especially not through soul-crushing despotism. We need to return to the great anti-totalitarian wisdom of the twentieth century so that we don't lose sight of these essential truths. Human nature can never be fundamentally changed, all three would agree. But while firmly and unequivocally castigating utopian and ideological "bloody and physical revolutions," and their accompanying "socialist projects" that led to violence and lies on an unprecedented level, Solzhenitsyn holds out hope for a "moral revolution" over the historical horizon that might elevate our souls while adding moral content to our precious political

[96]

and civil liberties. But he concedes that this is a "new phenomenon which we have yet to discover, discern, and bring to life." One might speak of the *bon usage* of utopia that at the same time acknowledges that theocracy and despotism do nothing to protect and promote the things of the spirit. Solzhenitsyn always insisted, as in the 1978 Harvard Commencement Address and elsewhere, that there could be a despotism in the name of the soul just as an inordinate attention to material concerns could distort human freedom and well-being. He was a partisan of *mesure*, or moderation, an equitable balancing of material and spiritual concerns. This is, of course, faithful to the best classical and Christian wisdom. And it has nothing to do with religious fanaticism.

A Past That Isn't Even Past

These efforts to think beyond the limits of our shapeless, decaying, postmodern, and relativistic democracies are useful and necessary. But they quickly come across their own limits. Russia has freed itself from the worst evils of ideological despotism (whatever its contemporary critics say) even as it lives with its powerful residues and unacceptable levels of private and public corruption. The Church is coming to life again and regularly pays tribute to the thousands of new martyrs who perished under Communism. Until recently one could read and speak freely on almost all subjects, and though criticizing the highest authorities is not without risk, books are available from every point of view, and no state-imposed lies are obligatory as in the Soviet days. Moreover, Solzhenitsyn's *The Gulag Archipelago*, the greatest anti-totalitarian work of all time, is required reading in Russian high schools. Russia has come a long way but it still has a very long way to go. In recent years, however, there has been an increasing brutality in public and private life as well as a growing tendency to assimilate the Soviet era into the Russian tradition *tout court*. Moreover, authoritarianism in Russia has grown considerably harsher since the invasion of Ukraine in February 2022, and even modest forms of opposition tend to be conflated with unpatriotic "extremism." A return to the path of civic freedom most likely

[97]

are fiercely denounced in the Western press as fascists, homophobes, and theocrats. And the absurd claim is made that the Polish moral conservatives threaten fundamental public liberties. With the return to power in late 2023 of Donald Tusk's Europhiles, the "rainbow coalition" of left-center parties, Poland faces significant retribution against conservative power in Polish politics and society. European elites cheerlead efforts to "save" Polish democracy by purging Polish life of any significant conservative presence. In their view, if democracy means anything, it must be "progressive democracy" or nothing at all. There is something Orwellian about this scenario.

In Hungary, a talented statesman of impeccable anti-totalitarian credentials, Viktor Orbán, is dismissed as a hater and tyrant for refusing to open Hungary to limitless Islamic immigration (and this in a small, vulnerable nation of just under ten million people). By openly and unapologetically defending the Christian mark of Europe, he has become anathema throughout Western quarters. And he is denounced as an anti-Semite for vigorously opposing George Soros's vision of an open—i.e. borderless and relativistic—society. Soros, to be sure, is a nonreligious Jew, one who has little or nothing good to say about Israel or traditional biblical morality. But the same Orbán respects public liberties, wins free elections, and has repudiated the once-racist and anti-Semitic Jabbok party. As Christopher Caldwell noted in the *Claremont Review of Books*,[7] Orbán's Hungary has passed a law against Holocaust denial, reopened major Jewish cultural sites, and established excellent bilateral relations with Israel. Jews are undoubtedly much safer in Budapest than in Paris or Marseilles today. Indeed, can Orbán really be driven out of the human race for holding positions that were widely shared in the West until quite recently and are still held by many decent citizens? Europe's establishment hates Christian conservatives and traditional patriots much more than it rejects or opposes former Communists. Legutko's remarks do much to explain this strange and ominous inversion, the perverse preference of Western elites for ex-Communists over patriotic and religious-minded conservatives, however democratic they may be.

So let us return to the enduring wisdom to be discerned from the great anti-totalitarians who inspired the revolution of 1989 and the accompanying, and slightly later, collapse of Communist totalitarianism in the USSR. As the distinguished French political theorist Philippe Bénéton has summarized this tragic (but by no means hopeless) wisdom, the "worst is always possible." This qualified pessimism was shared by all the great anti-totalitarians of the twentieth century, secular or religious. Bénéton adds that we learn from the great dissidents that "living in truth is a requirement of the natural law." One can add that the totalitarian negation of the distinction between truth and falsehood, good and evil, provided powerful verification—existential verification—for the law in the heart of men that Saint Paul appeals to in the Epistle to the Romans (2:15).

The experience of ideological revolution teaches us that all forms of Manichæism that claim to know with certitude who is a victim and who is a victimizer, lack self-knowledge, political prudence, and spiritual wisdom. As I have suggested more than once, this insight is best conveyed by Solzhenitsyn in *The Gulag Archipelago*. In a particularly memorable passage he writes that

> the line separating good and evil passes not through states, nor between classes, nor between political parties either—but right through every human heart—and through all human hearts. This line shifts. Inside us, it oscillates within the years…. It is impossible to expel evil from the world in its entirety, but it is possible to contract it within each person.[8]

Words of wisdom for the ages, and very relevant as an angry politically correct moralism (paradoxically rooted in dogmatic relativism) takes hold in the Western world. We in the West need to draw on the best anti-totalitarian wisdom, as never before.

Between utopian mendacity and postmodern moral indifference, lies this path of spiritual and political elevation that aims to bring together, slowly but surely, politics and conscience, freedom and moral self-limitation, with a healthy respect for human limits and imperfections. It is an arduous path that has nothing to do with false hopes and utopian illusions. Such wisdom is at the heart of the spirit of 1989, rightly understood. It is time to recover it before it is too late.

Sources and Suggested Readings

MY NARRATIVE of the events of 1989 in East-Central Europe is indebted to Duncan White, *Cold Warriors: Writers Who Waged the Literary Cold War* (New York: Harper Collins, 2019).

ALEKSANDR SOLZHENITSYN's seminal, and widely misunderstood "Letter to the Soviet Leaders" can be found in Solzhenitsyn, *East and West* (New York: Harper Perennial, 1980), 73–142. I have drawn on the crucial section entitled "Ideology," 120–29. See also chapter 3, "The Persistence of the Lie: The Totalitarian Impulse Old and New."

FOR MY DISCUSSION of Havel, I have drawn on his crucial dissident essays, such as "The Power of the Powerless," as well as his chapter "Politics, Morality and Civility" from Havel, *Summer Meditations* (New York: Alfred A. Knopf, 1992). This luminous chapter is a defining expression of his moral and political philosophy. Duncan White's lucid summary of Havel's thought and action was also quite helpful.

POPE JOHN PAUL II's fullest account of the nation and its natural and Christian roots can be found in Pope John Paul II, *Memory and Identity: Conversations at the Dawn of a Millennium* (New York: Rizzoli, 2005), especially 57–87. The memorable quotation about the dangers of slavishly following the culture of the contemporary West can be found on 143–44.

FOR AN INSIGHTFUL DISCUSSION of the crucial role of ideology in the legitimation of Communism right to the bitter end, see Timothy Garton Ash, *The Magic Lantern* (New York: Random House, 1990), 137.

ON RECENT, disturbing developments in Poland, see Daniel J. Mahoney, " 'Progressive Democracy' Strikes Back," at *The American Mind*, February 22, 2024.

ON THE RELENTLESS ASSAULTS on Orbán's Hungary, see Kevin J. McNamara, "How America's European Allies Got Stuck in a Foreign Policy Triangle," *National Interest* (August 16, 2019) and Christopher Caldwell, "Hungary and the Future of Europe," *Claremont Review of Books*, vol. 19, no. 2, (Spring 2019), 57–63. For a more recent account, see also Daniel J. Mahoney, "The Budapest Option," *The American Mind*, April 21, 2023.

I HAVE DRAWN FREELY on Aleksandr Solzhenitsyn's "An Orbital Journey," a profound speech delivered in Zurich on May 31, 1974, on the occasion of receiving the Golden Matrix Prize of the Italian Catholic Press Union. It appeared in English for the first time at *National Review* on line, January 7, 2019, with a preface by Daniel J. Mahoney. It is Solzhenitsyn's most philosophical and suggestive discussion of modernity and its discontents.

AT THE END of this chapter, I have drawn on a private correspondence with Philippe Bénéton with his kind permission.

CHAPTER 9

THE 1619 PROJECT: RACIALISM
AS A NEW FORM OF THE LIE

L ET US TURN now from the (lost) promise of 1989 to a discussion of the new racialism, the latest and most virulent expression of the Ideological Lie, and of "systematic" self-loathing, to invent a phrase. To repeat: A self-respecting people must be a self-critical people, open to introspection and ready to repent of real sin. But self-criticism is not the same as self-loathing. Reckless and willful distortion of the historical record betokens not integrity, but ingratitude toward those who have left the American people a noble, if imperfect, civic and moral inheritance. The 1619 Project represents everything to be avoided in this regard. It is an effort to identify the American story unilaterally with irredeemable racism, systematic oppression, unprecedented violence, and Hitlerian malignity. It is a matter of a civic narrative that has no place for civic comity, repentance, redemption, reframing, or self-correction. It is ideological through and through.

The 1619 Project first appeared in a special issue of *The New York Times Magazine* dated August 14, 2019. At that time, it comprised a series of articles on a theme outlined by the black journalist and activist Nikole Hannah-Jones in her flagship essay, "America Wasn't a Democracy, Until Black Americans Made It One." In 1619, a ship arrived at Point Comfort, Virginia, "bearing a cargo of twenty to thirty enslaved Africans." Hannah-Jones sought to make that landing into America's founding moment, eclipsing the Pilgrim settlements and the Mayflower Compact (1620), the Declaration of Independence (1776), the Constitutional Convention (1787), and the "new birth of freedom" heralded by Abraham Lincoln in the Gettysburg Address (1863). To the 1619 Project, slavery is more than America's "original sin": it is a moral stain that the nation can never escape or overcome. No subsequent developments truly matter. America is a nation with the soul of a "forced-labor camp," as Hannah-Jones repeatedly calls plantations like Thomas Jefferson's Monticello. Whites are ontologically guilty, and blacks seemingly can do no wrong (except those free-thinking blacks who depart from the obligatory neoracialist narrative).

This effort to valorize recrimination and prohibit civic reconciliation was lauded by journalists, racial activists, "progressive" educators, "woke" capitalists, and one of our two major political parties. Hannah-Jones was awarded a Pulitzer Prize, and the 1619 Project was quickly adopted as the basis of history and civic curriculums in school systems across the country. Charles R. Kesler pointed out in a *New York Post* op-ed (June 19, 2020) that the mayhem that overtook many American cities after George Floyd's death was inspired by the inconsolable hatred Hannah-Jones preaches. The riots of summer 2020, according to Kesler, are thus best understood as the "1619 riots." In a tweet that quickly followed (and was just as quickly removed), Hannah-Jones enthusiastically agreed. Strikingly, however, she denied that the willful destruction of property, broken windows, and arson had anything to do with violence. "Violence," in her view, is the unique prerogative of whites. Other contributors to the "project," especially Leslie Alexander and Michelle Alexander, go out of their way to minimize the violence that accompanied the mass demonstrations in summer 2020. They paint a picture of "brutal" police attacking "peaceful protesters," an account of events that strains credulity.[1]

The project's willful distortions of fact have received criticism from many corners. Distinguished scholars such as James M. McPherson (perhaps the greatest living historian of the Civil War), Sean Wilentz (a liberal patriot of the first order), CUNY history professor James Oakes, and award-winning historian Gordon S. Wood challenged Hannah-Jones's lies and distortions, her tendentious ideology, and her absurd claim that Americans asserted their independence from Great Britain in order to preserve chattel slavery against abolitionists in the mother country. The community activist Robert Woodson (already mentioned in the first chapter of this book) founded 1776 Unites, a broad coalition of black thinkers, activists, and ministers (as well as independent-minded liberals and secularists) who, as their name suggests, reiterated their commitment to the principles of the Declaration of Independence. 1776 Unites emphasizes civic pride, moral agency, and the self-respect of black Americans who will not stoop to partake in a debilitating cult of racial resentment and victimization.

The black political scientist Wilfred Reilly is an active participant in 1776 Unites. In a special January 2022 issue of *National Review*, Reilly firmly refuted the misrepresentations, half-truths, and often startling omissions that define the 1619 Project. As he argued, contributors to the project ignored the nuanced but deeply felt patriotism of most thinkers and activists, black and white, who fought to end slavery. These abolitionists did not reject or mock the principles of '76. To the contrary: they abhorred slavery *because* they affirmed the liberty and equality of all human beings under Nature's God. Reilly helpfully highlights a long lineage of black American patriots from Frederick Douglass, Booker T. Washington, and Martin Luther King Jr. to Robert Woodson and Thomas Sowell. The implication is clear: America cannot be healed by men and women who hate their country, loathe its principles, and see nothing but racism in its most noble truths and affirmations.

But these many eloquent objections have not stopped Hannah-Jones and her collaborators from distributing their message all over America, with the help of lavish funding and public honors. *The 1619 Project: A New Origin Story* is now available in a beautifully printed and produced volume that expands the original contributions, adds new essays and themes, and includes a large admixture of poetry and fiction to accompany the prose essays. No doubt in response to the criticism described above, the essays are occasionally more nuanced than the originals. But the broad emphases remain the same, and the ideological Manichæism remains dominant as ever. There is a marginally greater willingness to acknowledge that Abraham Lincoln was antislavery (although incorrigibly racist, see *1619*, 23–25), and the contributors ever so slightly qualify the claim that the American Revolution was fought to preserve race-based slavery. Mostly, though, Hannah-Jones responds to her critics not with good arguments but with predictable indignation and ad hominems. In an introductory preface, she confesses herself shocked that a "small group of historians attempted to discredit" the 1619 Project, as if she expected that her anti-American slander would receive nothing but praise. And in response to Lincoln scholar Allen Guelzo's observation that she launched her crusade from a position of "ultimate cultural privilege," Hannah-Jones calls Guelzo—of course—a racist (1619, xxxvi). Like the ideologist she is, Hannah-Jones does everything to chase off the conversation before it has the chance to begin.

The packaging is undoubtedly prettier, but the assault on America— and on the excellence and dignity of our political principles—is as sustained and unqualified as ever. The immense sacrifices of the Union soldiers, in lives or limbs, count for nothing in this volume: the boys in blue, too, were incorrigible racists, and anyway the slaves basically freed themselves. Similarly, banning the slave trade in 1808—as allowed or even encouraged by the Federal Constitution of 1787—was no great achievement. In fact, she argues, it may have been motivated by a racist desire to keep the black population from overwhelming the white population in key states of the Deep South.

A foundational conceit of this book is that Americans are denied access to the most fundamental truths about American history and the racial oppression that animates it. Hannah-Jones wants us to believe that unless her work is in every elementary school and coffee shop, Americans will never learn about the horrors of slavery, which endure to this day. But her account of what American students learn in school is unrecognizable to me. Nonstop attention to slavery, Jim Crow, and the secular religion of race- and gender-based "diversity" has been the norm in American schools for a very long time now. In truth, students already come away with little sense that there are elements of the American experience *not* tainted by racism.

In her preface, Hannah-Jones expresses her dismay that graduating high-school students cannot, when polled, name many essential facts about slavery and the causes of the Civil War (1619, xx). But as any experienced teacher these days will readily attest, students can tell you little or nothing about almost *any* major historical or political phenomenon. My students do not know that Communist regimes killed nearly one hundred million human beings in the twentieth century and unleashed a persecution of religion unprecedented in human history. The humorist Ben Stein once wrote amusingly (in *The American Enterprise* magazine) about an intern of his from UCLA, a major university and not the worst of the lot, who was outraged when she discovered that the Japanese had attacked Pearl Harbor. Stein had to reassure her that we had fought and won a war in response to the attack and that the Japanese were now our allies.

Another of Hannah-Jones's major objectives is to recharacterize Abraham Lincoln, the Great Emancipator, as an irredeemable racist (*1619*, 23–25). She lifts select quotations almost wholly out of context to portray him as a fraud who had nothing but contempt for black people. Her preface focuses on just one meeting with black leaders in 1862, during which the president entertained the question of sending freed blacks to colonies outside the United States. The reader would not know that Lincoln talked about anything else but colonization, or that he quickly abandoned the idea and fought instead for "a new birth of freedom," as he called it in the Gettysburg Address, on the American continent.

This kind of lazy polemic is nothing new. Contemporary ideologues also labor to cancel Lincoln for his supposed racism, as, for example, when he told Illinois farmers that though it was grievously wrong to enslave a black woman, they did not have to marry one. A more measured student of politics and history, attentive to the arts of civic and moral prudence, might discern the underlying antiracist intent at work here. With his distinction between enslavement and marriage, Lincoln was pressing his countrymen to recognize the true nature of equality: again and again he stressed that black men and women, however any Southerner might feel about them personally, were children of God. They were thus endowed with the natural right to keep what they earned "by the sweat of their brow." Hannah-Jones dismisses all this, as well as anything else that might do credit to Lincoln's name. The Emancipation Proclamation, the arming of free blacks to fight courageously for Union and liberty, and Lincoln's last major address in 1865 calling for the gradual extension of suffrage to freed blacks in Louisiana are either brushed over in passing or ignored completely. Lincoln is unquestionably guilty, and no empirical evidence to the contrary can prove otherwise.

This character assassination is expertly refuted in Mary Grabar's *Debunking the 1619 Project: Exposing the Plan to Divide America.*[2] Dr. Grabar is a former English instructor at Emory University who previously exposed the falsehood of another anti-American historian in *Debunking Howard Zinn* (2019). Her newest book provides the most comprehensive critique of the 1619 Project to date. The best chapter, "Taking Down Abraham Lincoln," lays out Lincoln's true positions regarding union and liberty, racism and slavery (*Debunking*, 193–232). For Lincoln, slavery was loathsome because it said to the slave: "*You work* and toil and earn bread, and I'll *eat* it." This, the rail-splitter could never abide. Grabar appreciates that as a statesman Lincoln had to negotiate with "free soil" Northerners who really were racist *and* antislavery. Through the art of prudence, he needed to renew the American people's fidelity to their highest moral and civic principles. That was the crucial first step.

Hannah-Jones also remakes Frederick Douglass in her own image, characterizing him as an unremittingly bitter critic of Lincoln (*1619*, 25). But Grabar shows that this, too, is false. Douglass called Lincoln his friend, recognizing that the president had treated him with great respect. He acknowledged that Lincoln "loathed slavery," though prudence held him back from eradicating it as swiftly and unilaterally as Douglass would have liked. Douglass shared Lincoln's conviction that the Constitution of 1787 was a "GLORIOUS LIBERTY DOCUMENT, one that in its core principles and its refusal to mention or validate 'the hateful thing' that was slavery, sustained the cause of freedom" (*Debunking*, 217–21). As Grabar points out, Douglass was "filled with grief" (*Debunking*, 224) upon learning of Lincoln's assassination.

But one would learn nothing about these truly decisive facts if one depended upon either the first or the more recent iteration of the 1619 Project. The contributors to the project quote extremely selectively from Douglass's famous speech on July 5, 1852 ("What to the Slave is the Fourth of July"). That speech contains stern and justified condemnation of slavery's moral evil, but also admiration for the courage and genius of America's founders. To omit the second part of the speech from any account of Douglass's views is dishonesty of the first order. As Grabar suggests, students need to study all parts of Douglass's speech, as well as the deep thought underlying Lincoln's principled and passionate opposition to chattel slavery (*Debunking*, 216–22). There is more to Lincoln than a single meeting with black leaders in 1862. But Hannah-Jones prefers to denounce rather than to understand. Self-righteousness is easy for those who wear ideological blinders.

The rest of the essays in the collection (eighteen in all) are no better. UPenn law professor Dorothy Roberts simply takes for granted that Jefferson fathered children with his slave Sally Hemings, ignoring persistent reasons for doubt (*1619*, 52). She describes abortion on demand, which has ravaged black communities, as a requirement of antiracism (along with a whole slew of counterproductive statist policies) (*1619*, 60). Princeton sociologist Matthew Desmond, for his part, identifies slavery with capitalism (*1619*, 181). He tells us that a truly antiracist America must also be a socialist one. But are there no similarities between the paternalism of the slave plantation and the despotism of many state-socialist systems? Our neo-Marxist ideologues refuse to differentiate free labor and free economic initiatives from the system of cruel racial domination that informed economic arrangements under slavery. In doing so, they willfully ignore the incompatibility of slavery with the sustained economic development that is the hallmark of a genuine market economy.

Capitalism helped *end* slavery, not create it. As Milton Friedman demonstrated in *Capitalism and Freedom* (1962), a businessman who refuses to do business with a black family is letting racial prejudice impede him from conducting profitable trade in a humane and civilized way. The Baron de Montesquieu had already made this point in Book

[109]

XX of *The Spirit of the Laws,* the first of two books dedicated to discussing the humanizing and liberating effects of free commerce. Such commerce cures destructive prejudices every day. In a famous passage near the end of *Democracy in America,* volume 1, Alexis de Tocqueville contrasted the hustle and bustle of men at work in the free state of Ohio with the "half-deserted fields" and sluggish lethargy in the slave state of Kentucky (*DA,* 331–33). A political order that actively promotes free commercial arrangements is in principle antithetical to race-based chattel slavery. We have known this truth for nearly four centuries, although our academic Marxists will deny it in spite of the abundant evidence. Today, Nigerians, Ghanaians, many Caribbean blacks, Indians from the Indian subcontinent, Asians, and Jews economically *outperform* white Americans—making it hard to sustain the argument that we live in a neoapartheid state devoid of opportunity for "people of color."

New York Times columnist Jamelle Bouie, contributing a chapter on "Politics," gives a reasonably accurate account of Senator John C. Calhoun's despicable views on slavery as a "positive good" and blacks as "ignorant, degraded, and vicious" (*1619,* 202). Yet he cannot see that both Lincoln and Ulysses S. Grant adamantly opposed such un-American and un-Christian views. That is why they fought a long, bloody Civil War to its successful conclusion: to ensure that the Confederate States of America, committed to some version of Calhoun's position, could not perpetuate itself. Bouie is keen to show that Calhoun's view somehow survives in the person of Donald Trump, whom he associates with the most vicious and demagogic racism (*1619,* 208). He does not seem to think he needs evidence for this claim, or for his assertion that commonsense voter regulations are part of a broader scheme to oppress and disenfranchise black Americans. Bouie himself is a vulgar practitioner of racialist demagoguery.

Evidence, in general, is in short supply in these essays—one contributor simply assumes that Democratic Senator Daniel Patrick Moynihan only fretted over the state of fatherless black families as a backhanded means of blaming black mothers for the problems in the black community (*1619,* 208). Over and over again, ideologically charged accusations substitute for reasoned discussion. University of Pennsylvania Professor Anthea Butler writes under the heading of "Church," but the only Gospel she can esteem is that of Marxism and "Black Liberation theology" (*1619*, 351). Celebrity demagogue Ibram X. Kendi refuses to acknowledge that any real "progress" has been made in American society regarding race and racism since 1865 (*1619*, 425). But is anything more racist than to suggest that white people have oppression built into their civic DNA? Indeed, the entire volume suggests that blacks, too, are essentially powerless to overcome a racism that is coextensive with America itself.

Another important new book provides a much-needed corrective to this bleak, falsified picture. In *1620: A Critical Response to the 1619 Project*,[3] former Boston University anthropology professor Peter W. Wood shows that the regime of chattel slavery took many decades or more to solidify after 1619 in Virginia and the rest of the South (*1620*, 38). Thus 1619 was not even the true founding of American slavery, let alone of America. Moreover, Wood shows the historical ubiquity of slavery itself: millions of Europeans were captured by Muslims in North Africa over several centuries; the Islamic slave trade was even more extensive and brutal than the Atlantic one; and conditions for slaves in Brazil were far deadlier than those in North America (*1620*, 44).

Using this context and perspective, Wood puts paid to one of the 1619 Project's most woefully irresponsible rhetorical tropes: its repeated comparisons between slavery in America and death camps in Nazi Germany (*1620*, 206). In the summer months, Wood points out, most slaves worked five and a half days a week. Some slaves became skilled artisans—a few even won their freedom, and a small number became wealthy. Some freed blacks owned slaves themselves (*1620*, 42). Wood stresses that chattel slavery was always a moral and civic abomination. But to point out that slave plantations in the United States did not resemble Nazi extermination camps is not to make an apology for slavery. It is simply to insist on historical honesty and the obligation of the historian and political analyst to make distinctions when necessary and appropriate.

Such honesty is at a disadvantage in our current climate. Near the end of his book, Wood wisely notes that teenagers "are by nature inclined to see hypocrisy everywhere in the adult world." The 1619 Project feeds this propensity by "giving full scope to a cynical reading of the American past," and, I might add, the American present. Such cynicism ignores the countless exemplars of "self-restraint, self-sacrifice, and commitment to the common good," in Wood's words, that have made the United States a morally estimable country, if an imperfect one. No study of 1619 is complete without 1620, the Puritan efforts to establish liberty under God, and—even more importantly—1776, 1787, 1863, and all they represent. If, concludes Wood, the young are taught the terrible falsehood that "racism is and always was the dominant ideology" then the American experiment will hang by the thinnest thread, and we will have no Lincolns to save it (*1620*, 206–07). Let us return to the "better angels of our nature," who teach salutary self-criticism and civic renewal, not self-loathing and despair.

Afterword: A Final Word on Wokeness and Racial Guilt

American Awakening,[4] a 2021 work by the Georgetown political theorist Joshua Mitchell, shows the way forward from the Ideological Lie in its racialist manifestations. Mitchell has written that rare book that captures the state of our souls and describes our situation with clarity, astuteness, and spiritual depth. *American Awakening* is a work that expertly combines classical political philosophy with penetrating cultural diagnosis in a manner that holds up a revealing mirror to the great afflictions of our time. At the same time, Mitchell admirably avoids narrow partisanship and undue polemics. His book deserves to be compared to such memorable achievements as Raymond Aron's *The Opium of the Intellectuals* (1955), Philip Rieff's *The Triumph of the Therapeutic* (1966), and Allan Bloom's *The Closing of the American Mind* (1987)—enduring works that combined theoretical penetration with analyses of our civilizational crisis.

Mitchell's subject is, in the words of his subtitle, "identity politics and other afflictions of our time." Readers expecting either accommodation to the regnant civil religion of "transgression and innocence" (*AA*, xii) or an angry ideological screed should look elsewhere. Mitchell aims higher. With impressive lucidity, he painstakingly examines a new secular religion that is profoundly indebted to Christianity while having "no place for the God who judges or the God who forgives" (*AA*, 41). Such an approach, he shows, is necessarily cruel, dogmatic, indiscriminate, and unforgiving. The partisans of identity politics reject both the Christian understanding of original sin—the observable fact that no human beings are born without sin and all stand in need of forgiveness and redemption—as well as what Mitchell suggestively calls "liberal competence," the confidence that individuals endowed with free will and conscience are moral agents who, with the appropriate education and encouragement, can make their way responsibly in the world as competent citizens and providers (*AA*, xxvi). The theoreticians of identity politics derive from Christianity a belief in an "invisible spiritual economy," but they understand that economy through a doctrinaire conception of transgression and innocence tied to *visible* groups who are guilty or innocent not because of what they have done but because of *who they are* (*AA*, xiv). White, heterosexual men, even "the least among" them, to echo the language of Scripture—the poor, the addicted, the downtrodden—are said to be essentially, ontologically *guilty* (*AA*, xvi). Blacks, women, and persons who identify with the ever-expanding ideological construction called LGBTQ+ are by definition innocent, and forever so, or so it is claimed. As Mitchell shows, the permanently guilty must resort to virtue signaling of the most demeaning sort if they are to avoid cancellation or other rituals associated with public humiliation. Not only God, but also forgiveness and the whole economy of mutual reconciliation and accountability, are thus absent from this "identity-politics accounting scheme" (*AA*, xvi–xviii).

Identity politics claims to be egalitarian, but in truth it radically separates human beings in a manner only previously seen in the totalitarian ideologies and regimes of the twentieth century. Identity politics sees no struggle between good and evil in every human heart, as in the classical and Christian understanding of free will, conscience, and moral responsibility. It has no place for the drama of human existence. Like the totalitarians of old, in numerous institutions in civil society, especially our universities, the new ideologues pronounce who is absolutely guilty and who is innocent and pure, with a monstrous self-assurance based on the visible signs of evil and injustice (e.g., whiteness and "heteronormativity"). Such a world—at once racialist and ideological—becomes a perverse spiritual despotism dominated by tyrannical ideological clichés that allow the woke to dispense with "the guilty" with remarkable impunity and cruelty. The old Christian anthropology cohered naturally with the requirements of liberal competence and civic responsibility, since in a "mixed world of purity and stain," imperfect human beings had to strive to "build a world together," doing their best to respect one another as persons made in God's image. Identity politics inexorably leads to soft and eventually not-so-soft despotism, as the ontologically guilty are swept away, and those who "cover themselves with the fig leaf of innocence" become the beneficiaries of an omnicompetent (and arbitrary) state that "allocate[s] resources to the innocents and to their causes" (*AA*, xx–xxvi).

Civic responsibility and moral accountability thus have no place in the ideological schemes put forward by the denizens of identity politics. Such a regime—and we are indeed in the process of creating a radically new political order—is at once anti-Christian (or antibiblical) and profoundly antiliberal. It wars with every aspect of our moral and civic inheritance. Mitchell thus intimates that religious believers, partisans of liberal competence, and conservative defenders of our moral and cultural inheritance must put aside their differences and come together to defend the conception of liberty and responsibility, under God, that properly undergirds a free society. This is the old American synthesis, and it remains eminently worth defending. It is open to men and women of all races since it alone affirms common humanity. There is in truth no viable alternative, no coherent anthropology or account of the human person, that can sustain liberty and human dignity in a free republic.

[114]

THE 1619 PROJECT: RACIALISM AS A NEW FORM OF THE LIE

Identity politics creates an atmosphere of division and disdain with more than its share of Orwell's ritualistic "Two Minutes Hate" from 1984. No one is truly protected from new rounds of repudiation and cancellation. New purge trials undoubtedly await those who play with ideological fire, since the innocent can become transgressors at the drop of a pin. Mitchell shows with great sensitivity that black Americans are among the principal victims of this new ideological dispensation: The "innocent" are always to be treated as "victims," as persons bereft of moral and political agency. Drawing on the insights of Robert Woodson (*AA*, 82, 98–99), Mitchell demonstrates how this newly dominant narrative hurts the most vulnerable by erasing all the "remarkable models of self-help" in black communities. Gone is the example of those "accomplishments of black entrepreneurs and mutual aid societies during the most brutal racial repression and slavery." Black intellectuals such as Woodson are treated as the enemy precisely because they defend a Christian view of sin and responsibility, an authentically liberal notion of civic competence and self-help, and proper pride in the capacity of black Americans to be self-governing citizens in the most capacious sense of that term. Look, Mitchell says, at what has happened to Booker T. Washington, whose message of determination and self-help is central to the restoration of liberal competence in communities racked by crime, violence, and despair (*AA*, 81–82). Washington, once a hero to black and white Americans alike, has become more or less a nonperson, dismissed out of hand by the guardians of ideological correctness as a racially subservient "Uncle Tom." This, too, hurts the "least among us" and substitutes permanent grievance for the faith in one's God-given gifts that allows a common world to be built and to flourish.

There is no shortage of memorable gems in Mitchell's inviting and challenging book. He has choice words to say about the "bipolarity" of the young, torn between unreasonable expectations that they can change the world, and fear of the most humanizing face-to-face encounters with other human beings. He ably chronicles the numerous "substitutes," as he calls them, that we late moderns turn to—drugs of all sorts, among them—to find happiness divorced from competence and responsibility. In doing so, he redeems political philosophy as the truly "architectonic science," as Aristotle famously called it, the one that knows the city and soul in the most comprehensive way. In *American Awakening*'s final words, Mitchell reminds us, in light of the panic that accompanied the coronavirus, that the "prudent wish to protect" lives has nothing to do with creating a "world freed from the curse of death," an essentially utopian aim that infantilizes free men and women by aiming to create a world without risk or responsibility, with no higher or nobler goal than self-preservation (*AA*, 228–38). It is a world where we defer in a supine way to self-described "experts" and prohibit public worship while permitting allegedly "essential" pursuits. It is progressive managerialism posing as democracy and good government. It is as foul as Tocqueville's insidious "tutelary despotism" of a schoolmaster state that enervates the soul and undermines our capacity to govern ourselves thoughtfully and responsibly.

Joshua Mitchell has written an anti-totalitarian classic in the guise of a critique of identity politics (although his book very powerfully provides that service, too). The essential lesson is clear: There is no liberty, human dignity, or moral and civic responsibility without a clear recognition that the "line dividing good and evil cuts through the heart of every human being," in Solzhenitsyn inestimable worlds that we have had ample reason to recur to throughout this book. To deny that elementary moral fact is to negate the foundations of a free society—and to succumb to the Ideological Lie at the heart of every totalitarian regime and ideology. Mitchell's welcome book shows us precisely what is at stake in the racialist version of the Lie.

Sources and Suggested Readings

IN ADDITION to the Grabar and Wood books cited in the body of the text, I highly recommend Coleman Hughes's cogent and humane plea for Americans to remain faithful to the non-negotiable ethical principle that human beings should be judged by "the content of their character" and not "the color of their skin." For his particularly compelling critique of neo-racism, see Hughes, *The End of Race Politics: Arguments for a Colorblind America* (New York: Thesis, 2024).

MILTON FRIEDMAN demonstrates with rare clarity that racial discrimination is incompatible with the theory and practice of capitalism or the market economy. See Friedman, *Capitalism and Freedom* (Chicago: University of Chicago Press, 2022). The book was originally published in 1962.

FOR TOCQUEVILLE'S vivid and illuminating comparison of manners, morals, and economic vitality (and productivity) in the free state of Ohio and the slave state of Kentucky, respectively, see his *Democracy in America,* trans. and eds. Harvey C. Mansfield and Delba Winthrop (Chicago: University of Chicago Press, 2000), 331–33.

CHAPTER 10

MORAL INVERSION:
WHY RADICAL RELATIVISM LEADS
TO IDEOLOGICAL FANATICISM

I N OUR ERA, truth is under systematic assault from moralistic fanatics
who are at the same time thoroughgoing relativists and dyed-in-the-
wool subjectivists. The Catholic journalist Karlo Broussard put it well in
his recently published booklet, *The New Relativism*:

> *The fight against relativism is not over. The agents of relativism
> are still out there, seeking to fit the world to their own desires
> and likes rather than discover and understand the world in order
> to better conform to it. And they do it under the guise of 'woke'
> absolutes, which on face value seem true and good, but in reality
> mean the opposite of what an unsuspecting person might think.*[1]

The fervid intensity of the woke absolutists, their anger and excoriation,
should not be mistaken for a commitment to truth and truth-seeking.
Their indignation, their aim to cancel—to morally obliterate—those
they cannot abide is a consequence of the fact that they have left the
world of objective truth and measured moral judgment behind.

At the same time, these vehement enemies of Truth with a capital T
do not hesitate to accuse their opponents of departing from the only ac-
ceptable narratives regarding ubiquitous white racism, the self-evidence
of gender theory, the grave threat to democracy posed by conservative
populists and moral traditionalists, and the unquestionable need to genuflect before the authority of "Science" as redefined by politically correct
elites. Their censorious appeal to truth (i.e. their ideological agenda) is
thus at the service of intellectual and political authoritarianism (itself at
the service of sexual and sociopolitical liberationism). These self-evident

goods justify all efforts to silence those who still affirm that *"freedom is ordered to the truth* and is fulfilled in man's quest for truth and in man's living in the truth," as Pope John Paul II put it in his address to the United Nations General Assembly on October 5, 1995. Paradoxically, the moralistic indignation shared by totalitarians in the twentieth century and woke fanatics in the twenty-first is primarily directed against those who, in Pope John Paul II's words, still uphold the "moral structure of freedom," or what Pope Benedict XVI called the "moral ecology" rooted in conscience and truth that alone can give form and life to human liberty. Human beings have a nature, and we forget that elementary truth at our peril.

Ideological fanaticism is the inevitable consequence of a nihilistic denial of an order of things, of a natural moral order available to human beings through reason and experience. The willful denials of truth and falsehood, good and evil, virtue and vice, understood as fundamental distinctions rooted in the structure of reality, inevitably lead to a comprehensive subversion of all the goods of human life: of liberty, the life of the mind, sound politics, and moral judgment. Human beings are moral as well as political animals, and the denial of these basic truths does not abolish moral phenomena as much as distort them or cause them to live a diminished and zombie-like existence. In what follows, with the help of the twentieth-century Anglo-Hungarian political philosopher and philosopher of science Michael Polanyi, I aim to highlight the "moral inversion" common to modern totalitarianism and the postmodern nihilism from which woke activism is almost wholly derivative. Such moral inversion is defined by a mix of "official" relativism and fanatical moral indignation, rooted in the ideological rejection of a natural order of things and of a shared public or common world, where our manifold responsibilities and duties first come to sight.

Radical Liberals and Illiberal Radicals

Polanyi develops a deeply illuminating description and dissection of nihilistic "moral inversion" in his 1958 masterwork *Personal Knowledge: Towards a Post-Critical Theory*, a work that aims to recover an ontologically and morally realist account of scientific inquiry and moral judgment freed from the limits of positivism and open to the various forms of "tacit knowing" available to thinking and acting man. His clearest and fullest account of the link between moral nihilism and ideological fanaticism, however, is found in a chapter entitled "Perils of Inconsistency" in an earlier book entitled *The Logic of Liberty*, first published by the University of Chicago Press in 1951.[2] This chapter amply rewards close examination.

To begin with, Polanyi is particularly sensitive to the tensions, or even contradictions, at the heart of liberal theory and practice. As Pierre Manent has noted, a few early modern liberals such as John Milton in his *Areopagitica* saw political, intellectual, and religious liberty as crucial preconditions for attaining truth. But early modern liberalism, or protoliberalism, was haunted by "philosophical doubt," since it was first and foremost motivated by what Polanyi calls a "detestation for religious fanaticism" of the kind that had led to the wars of religion (*LL*, 116–17). The theoretical radicalism and the underlying antireligious ire of such liberalism was for a long time muted in the Anglo-American world, as liberal constitutionalism in England and America aimed primarily to pacify religious contestation without affirming radical moral skepticism or upholding a civically corrosive neutrality between belief and unbelief. Even Locke refused toleration to atheists since they were, in Polanyi's words, "socially unreliable" (*LL*, 117). Locke's epistemic skepticism was, of course, acidic enough. It contributed to the nihilistic skepticism of the French encyclopedists, as Father John Courtney Murray rightly argues in his 1960 classic, *We Hold These Truths* (Pierre Manent makes the same case in his 1994 book, *The City of Man*). But for a very long time the "consummation" of this deep tension within liberalism was, in Polanyi's words, held at bay "in the Anglo-American region by an instinctive reluctance to pursue the accepted philosophical premises to their ultimate conclusions" (*LL*, 121). Similarly, utilitarian philosophy was a thin and arid substitute for true moral judgment. But utilitarians and philosophical empiricists nonetheless pretended that their hedonic premises gave support to ethical behavior as wise

[121]

"maxims of prudence" (*LL*, 121–22). This was, to be sure, spiritually thin gruel. But it was *not yet* politically corrosive, at least in any obvious or immediate sense.

Things took a different turn in continental Europe. There, liberalism quickly morphed into full-fledged radical skepticism as well as a penchant for revolutionary politics. As we have had reason to observe, the French Revolution revealed a fanaticism all its own, inspired by the hedonism and skepticism of the *philosophes*, the scientism and antireligious fury that were hallmarks of the continental Enlightenment, and by a "literary politics," as Alexis de Tocqueville phrased it, that aimed to design a wholly new political order from scratch, as if one were writing a play with a preordained happy ending. "Be my brother or I will kill you!" one prominent French aristocrat-turned-revolutionary proclaimed. The French Revolution may have given way to more orderly Napoleonic despotism, but revolutionary impatience only grew in fury in its aftermath.

Realism Against the Real

Polanyi expertly exposes the Achilles heel of European rationalism. In its disdain for priests and the Catholic religion, it took aim at everything that was allegedly unscientific, indemonstrable, and uncertain, including traditional morality. This was its salto mortale. To be sure, ethical principles are by no means arbitrary since, as persons, we know them through "participation" and lived experience. We can describe and evaluate virtues and vices in perfectly reasonable ways, as Aristotle and Saint Thomas so convincingly demonstrated. In addition, conscience, as described by Saint John Henry Newman, gives us access "to the rule of our conduct" and to the "standard of right and wrong" that commands obedience. For Newman, conscience additionally provided powerful evidence for the existence of God. It is indeed a "stern monitor" and should not be confused with subjectivism or the "right of self-will," as Newman so aptly put it. At the same time, as Polanyi suggests, our very real "obligations to tell the truth, to uphold justice and mercy" cannot be proved or demonstrated in a way that would satisfy the scientism of modern rationalists (*LL*, 120). A truncated Reason, irrationally but ardently affirmed, thus quickly becomes an enemy of the Real.

With the Marxism of Marx, the dialectic of skepticism and fanaticism begins to unleash its full fury. For Marx, the moral "superstructure" of society always and everywhere provides a groundless and hypocritical justification for class dominance and exploitation. As we have seen, in the second part of *The Communist Manifesto* Marx crudely mocks natural right or justice, along with any appeal, political, philosophical, or theological, to "eternal truths, such as Freedom, Justice, etc." (*LL*, 125). In prerevolutionary Russia, Marx's pseudoscientific socialism vied for attention with other subversive doctrines such as revolutionary populism and the overt and deadly nihilism so powerfully described by both Turgenev and Dostoevsky (*LL*, 128). In that milieu, the urge to negate and destroy took on the form of limitless moral passion, but one tied to philosophical and historical materialism, a materialism that has no place for authentic moral judgment or for salutary self-restraint. European revolutionaries such as the Bolsheviks and the Russian nihilists thus combined a sense of passionate righteousness with what Polanyi calls "scientific self-assurance" and an "impenetrable skepticism." This all culminated in "calculated brutality" (*LL*, 130).

We have now arrived at *moral inversion* proper. As Polanyi compellingly argues, with ideological despotism and its myriad practitioners and apologists, the "moral needs of man, which are denied expression in terms of human ideals, are injected into a system of naked power, to which they impart the force of blind moral passion" (*LL*, 131). The morally inverted, the ideologically fanatical, combine deep moral skepticism with the justification of the truly unjustifiable, such as revolutionary terror and unprecedented forms of tyranny. Moral inversion is one manifestation of what Aleksandr Solzhenitsyn called the "Ideological Lie," a term whose vital significance has been central to this book as a whole. Authentic moral aims are replaced by thoroughly ideological ones. The ideologist (and fellow-travelling intellectuals more broadly) act with the "whole force of his homeless moral passions within a purely materialistic framework of purposes" (*LL*, 131). A political, or rather, ideological order built on these mendacious claims destroys the moral integrity of those who succumb to it. It also makes genuine intellectual freedom impossible. When moral passions go completely underground and escape the tribunal of reasonable civic judgment, morality is transmogrified into moral destruction pure and simple. It reveals itself as pure *nothingness*. Reductive materialism, united with moralistic indignation and the messianic ideologies that aim to transform radically human nature and the only human condition we have known, can only deform reality and mutilate the bodies and souls of human beings. We have arrived at the Devil's work.

The Devil's Work

Let us turn to events closer to home. Even a cursory examination of contemporary intellectual life shows that the spirit of negation is alive among us, this time in the form of postmodern nihilism and its derivative: woke activism. In Roger Scruton's words, the new antinomians such as Michel Foucault could find in "social discourse" only the "voice of power."[3] *La pensée de soixante-huit* ("the thought of 1968"), as the French call it, could see in legitimate authority only authoritarianism, and of the most pernicious sort. What unhinged judgment they exhibited. In the age of ideological totalitarianism, of an unprecedently cruel tyranny, they saw the greatest and gravest of evils in "bourgeois domination." An "anatomist of power and the priest of liberation," as Scruton called him, Foucault and his epigoni, who quickly rose to the forefront in Western intellectual life, identified liberation or emancipation with cultural and political repudiation. This is the farthest thing from the affirmations of Pope John Paul II that I cited above.

This tumultuous revolt against decency, restraint, and humanizing authority has largely been "socialized" and institutionalized in our universities, cultural institutions, and newspaper boardrooms, as both Pierre Manent and Christopher Rufo have argued. A culture of civilizational self-loathing reigns supreme, or almost so. By denying that authority can

be exercised in humane, generous, and reciprocal ways, today's antinomians and woke activists see coercive power as the only way to "emancipate" victims (blacks, transsexuals, women, and the dispossessed) from
the "domination" that is coextensive with bourgeois society. They see
victims everywhere, and they adamantly reject moral agency and mutual
accountability as ways of promoting nonutopian justice and amicable
civic bonds. Woke despotism is thus the latest form of totalitarian moral
inversion, nearly identical in structure and form to the earlier hybrids of
nihilism and fanaticism that Polanyi described in the 1950s.

For his part, Scruton saw a Satanic impulse at work in these com-
plementary projects of cultural, political, and spiritual negation. As he
writes in his book *An Intelligent Person's Guide to Modern Culture*, first
published in 2000 and already cited in the introduction to this book,
those who relentlessly attempt to negate and repudiate our precious
moral, cultural, and civilizational inheritances are doing "the Devil's
work."[4] Scruton liked to remind his readers of Goethe's unnerving but
altogether compelling description of Mephistopheles in his masterpiece
Faust: "The spirit that forever negates!/ And rightly so: since everything
created,/ In turn deserves to be annihilated." There in a nutshell is the
effectual truth of the unrelenting postmodern project of cultural and
spiritual deconstruction. It is nothing less than a perverted effort to
undo God's creation.

Writing in 1951, Polanyi hoped against hope that the liberal order
could escape this deadly mix of debilitating doubt and moral inversion
by coming to terms with an older wisdom, including the wisdom of the
Catholic Church. Confronted by totalitarianism, he believed true liberals are those "who recognize transcendental obligations and are resolved
to preserve a society built on the belief that such obligations are real." In
doing so, they would discover the sobering truth that "they stand much
closer to believers in the Bible and in the Christian revelation, than to
the nihilist regimes, based on radical disbelief" (*LL*, 134). Ideological
fanaticism was the intermediate state that connected debilitating doubt
to pure negation.

Nothing has transpired since 1951 to invalidate Polanyi's intuitions and arguments, and developments closer to home confirm the urgent need for a high-minded reconciliation between modern liberty and a philosophically minded Christianity. But, alas, the kind of conservative liberalism that Polanyi so ardently hoped for is on life support, despite its formidable theoretical and practical merits.

And the Christian churches, even the Roman Catholic Church, are fast succumbing to the temptation to genuflect before the zeitgeist rather than renewing the "moral structure of freedom" so nobly and truthfully articulated by Pope John Paul II at the United Nations in October 1995. Some even evoke a new "age of the Spirit," where unchanging truth and the moral law give way to spurious theological enthusiasm and "signs of the times" ideologically construed. But the old verities persist, and they must be artfully articulated and vigorously defended in this age as in any other. Reconnecting truth and politics requires a dual, dialectical critique of both relativism and ideological fanaticism to which it gives rise.

Sources and Suggested Readings

POLANYI'S MASTERWORK, *Personal Knowledge: Towards a Post-Critical Theory* (Chicago: University of Chicago Press, 2015), carefully distinguishes the "personal" dimensions of the pursuit of truth from every form of deep relativism or subjectivism.

SAINT JOHN HENRY NEWMAN'S *A Letter to the Duke of Norfolk* (Rome: Aeterna Press, 2015) continues to provide the most thoughtful and authoritative critique of any identification of moral conscience with subjectivism or the "right to self-will."

CHAPTER 11

A TIME FOR COURAGE AND MODERATION

THE INHERITANCE WE defend—that noble civilizational patrimony that helps define the West and America—is not good simply because it is old or because it is ours. Rather, it is good because it is wisdom tried and true. As a result, we know that we can never begin anew with some revolutionary "Year Zero." The destructive zealots and ideologues among the French Revolutionaries did that, displaying deadly contempt for Burke's more capacious understanding of a primordial contract that connects the living, the dead, and those yet to be born. As a tradition dedicated to human liberty, the Western tradition is dynamic and expansive, yet it has ample room for true pietas. As the French political philosopher Bertrand de Jouvenel wrote so eloquently and discerningly in his 1955 classic, *Sovereignty: An Inquiry into the Political Good*: "Every individual with a spark of imagination feels deeply indebted to many others, the living and the dead, the known and the unknown....The wise man knows himself for debtor, and his actions will be inspired by a deep sense of obligation."[1]

Reason and experience alike testify that men and women become monsters when they confuse themselves with gods beholden to nothing or no one. In our times that conceit has led to utopian dreams and murderous rage, or to petty souls who rest content with what Blaise Pascal vividly called "licking the earth." Real human freedom and dignity need to be nourished by a deep sense of obligation, starting with our forebears, without whom we would not be or have anything at all. Natural piety, however, is not solely focused on the past: it lifts our gaze further outside ourselves to the mysterious *givenness* of the natural order. It is open to the grace that lifts our spirits and allows us to experience the presence of the Living God. Only by acknowledging our considerable debts to our forebears, to ennobling tradition, and to the natural and divine sources of our dignity as human beings, are we rendered capable of achieving great and good things in our turn. In our time, humility and magnanimity, humble deference to God and legitimate civic pride, stand or fall together.

The phrase, "great and good," is at the heart of my 2022 book, *The Statesman as Thinker: Portraits of Greatness, Courage, and Moderation.*[2] Therein I argue that the twin virtues of magnanimity and moderation—greatness of soul and a deeply felt sense of obligation to truth, liberty, and conscience—go hand in hand. In the domain of action, what towers above and truly endures is the admittedly rare combination of honorable ambition and self-conscious self-limitation, where greatness and goodness coexist in (relative) harmony, if in some tension.

Against the culture of repudiation, we need to open our hearts and minds to greatness, rightly understood. George Washington was one such exemplar of noble, honorable, and morally serious ambition, which he yoked to the service of his fledgling country and the larger cause of civilized liberty. Across the Atlantic, Napoleon famously complained that his contemporaries wanted him to be another Washington: a great man willing to leave the stage and go home when his duty was done. This he could not do. Tocqueville said of Napoleon that he was as great as one could be without being good. That "without being good" was his Achilles heel, his fatal flaw. Closer to our day, Charles de Gaulle said that Napoleon severed greatness and moderation, a lesson that should be instructive for future generations. Writing in 1924, de Gaulle observed that the great man's "works of energy" fizzle out, or give rise to tragedy, when they are severed from the "rules of classical order." From an appreciation of the "limits marked out by human experience, common sense, and the law," truly magnanimous statesmanship learns the "sense of balance, of what is possible, of measure, which alone renders the works of energy durable and fecund."[3]

De Gaulle already saw this severing of greatness and measure at work in the Nietzscheanized military and political elites of Wilhelmine Germany. How much worse, however, was the contempt for decency, moderation, and the moral law that informed Hitler's monstrous "revolution of ni-hilism"! Communism, too, warred unrelentingly against all the human goods, all the precious achievements of civilization: against truth, against human liberty and dignity, against the very idea of natural right, and against the "enduring verities" that transcend class interests and revo-lutionary pretensions. The Nazi and Communist efforts to impose what Eric Voegelin memorably called mendacious "Second Realities" on the only human condition we know, gave rise to forms of murderous tyranny hitherto unimaginable. True conservatives—and old-fashioned liberals—are uniquely equipped to recognize the essential unity between these two totalitarian regimes. How sad—but how instructive—that "progres-sives" everywhere, and far too many among the young, still believe that Communism is "good in theory," and not a few believe that it is desirable in practice. The promise of 1989 is all but forgotten.

As a country and as a civilization, we have failed miserably in passing on the lessons of the twentieth century to new generations. Chief among those lessons was a great warning against ideological Manichæism, which locates evil not in the flawed human heart, but in suspect groups (e.g., the Jews, the kulaks, religious believers, the bourgeoisie, assorted class enemies). This is an invitation, indeed, a sure route, to Hell on earth.

The New Totalitarians

Today, thirty-five years after the annus mirabilis of 1989, we are observ-ing a repetition in new form of the Ideological Lie, the theme of this book. Progressives willfully see in imperfect but largely decent societies nothing but evil, injustice, and exploitation. Critical Race Theory and wokeness have replaced gratitude to our forebears and democratic self-respect, and new groups of people, alleged oppressors, are called to loathe themselves or to be banished from the civic and human com-munity. Such unrelieved contempt for our fellow citizens has nothing to do with justice, social or otherwise. Quite the contrary. It makes a mockery of the shared bonds that make free civic life possible, and it creates a fictive world of permanent victims and oppressors. And it is light years away from the affirmation of common humanity without which humane and decent human life becomes impossible.

In this book, I have repeatedly appealed to the lucid and elevating moral wisdom of Aleksander Solzhenitsyn. Faced with human nature in extremis in the Soviet Gulag, Solzhenitsyn rediscovered a truth central to classical and Biblical wisdom, as well as to the sober moral and political wisdom of our founding fathers: "It is impossible to expel evil from the world in its entirety, but it is possible to constrict it within each person" (*GA*, 312). To acknowledge this is to begin to find wisdom and self-knowledge, to reconnect wisdom and morality and to find the true grounds of political moderation.

In contrast, the woke—coercive moral and political fanatics to the core—renew the Ideological Lie in the name of fighting racial, ethnic, and sexual injustice. But they end up tyrannizing the soul, and polluting the public space with insidious and suffocating clichés, because they do not begin to understand the moral drama at work in every human soul. They only know how to negate and repudiate, to destroy the precious and fragile inheritance that has been passed on to us for our safekeeping. To meet this threat, we need new statesmen to arise—to be cultivated— among us. Pending that, each of us needs to have some "tincture" of the statesman in him or her. The gradual renewal of authentic liberal arts, civic, and religious education will, over time, allow "greatness of soul" to manifest itself in our minds.

With that said, people often ask me how we can renew the noble tradition of statesmanship represented by Solon and Cicero in antiquity, and by the likes of Burke, Washington, Lincoln, Churchill, de Gaulle, and Havel, closer to our time. The first thing to do, of course, is to study them. As it happens, that is what they themselves did. Cicero's *On Duties* is a truly inestimable work that shaped the moral and political imagination of the West until the late nineteenth century. As I describe in *The Statesman as Thinker*, Cicero's honorable statesman is equally distant from the Machiavellian Prince and the Nietzschean "Overman," contemptuous as they are of traditional moral wisdom and an ethic of self-restraint and honorable ambition. But neither is Cicero's statesman averse to the legitimate, tough-minded exercise of authority that repels contemporary humanitarians. Neither hard nor soft in his moral bearing, the true statesman takes his bearing from the *honestum*—the fine, the noble, the honorable—at the service of civilized liberty. Liberty's moral preconditions and purposes are the true statesman's lodestars.

This is the realistic yet high-minded framework of thought and action that our theorists of repudiation so mindlessly aim to bury. Instead of legitimate authority, instead of decent norms that serve a community of citizens, they see only implacable power: crude, oppressive, self-serving, and now, predictably, "racist" to the core. These secular priests see only domination where others rightly discern love, consent, community, and the bonds of affection, civic and familial. The "heresy of domination," as Roger Scruton so suggestively calls it in *An Intelligent Person's Guide to Modern Culture*, takes a partial truth—that authority can become authoritarian and domineering—and turns it into a fanatical obfuscation, a refusal to "accept that power is sometimes benign and decent, like the power of a loving parent, conferred upon the object of love."[4] The partisans of this heresy govern those social and cultural institutions that they have come to commandeer, such as the universities and the media, in the very manner they condemn. If they reduce the exercise of authority to the will to power, to domination and exploitation, why will their forays into governance be any different from the corrosive doctrine that they preach?

As I argue in the closing pages of *The Statesman as Thinker*, "Our task is to reaffirm the real in a spirit of gratitude for what has been passed on by our forebears as a precious gift." Only by "repudiating repudiation," by refusing the spiritually and civically corrosive path of negation, do we have a fighting chance of again seeing the meeting of wisdom and morality in our fragile and embattled civilization. But that act of moral recovery and civilizational renewal will demand an exercise of spiritual strength that will test our mettle as free and civilized men and women. True moderation will demand rare courage, not tepid passivity before the forces of self-loathing, negation, and repudiation. That is the "false, reptile prudence" that Edmund Burke saw at work among English Whigs who wanted to make their peace with Jacobinism. To cite the last sentence of my previous book, "the choice is ours." There is no reason to despair, because free will is a gift from on High. It is up to us to exercise it prudently, justly, and courageously—that is, wisely. It is up to us to reject the "inhumane reign of the Lie," as Pasternak called it, once and for all. To that common task, this book aims to make a significant contribution.

CONCLUSION:

A FINAL WORD TO THE LEFT, CENTER, AND RIGHT

THE AUTHOR OF this book is an unabashed conservative and unapologetically so. Without proper deference to our civilized patrimony, without the serious resolve to preserve, and reform, our common life in accord with the noble principles of justice imparted by our forebears, we will founder upon the shoals of nihilistic negation. Intentionally or not, we will impart to the young hatred, not love; despair, not hope; confusion, not self-confidence rooted in tried-and-true wisdom.

This author loves liberty of a "manly, moral, and regulated" kind, as Edmund Burke so eloquently put it at the beginning of his *Reflections on the Revolution in France*, the founding text of a modern conservatism committed to the preservation of ordered liberty. He is also an American patriot who cherishes our republican institutions and our constitutional forms. He remains committed to the "honorable determination" (*Federalist* No. 39) of a free people to vindicate the human capacity for self-government, to "liberty under God and the laws" as Alexis de Tocqueville so suggestively put it in *The Old Regime and the Revolution* (1856). To truly love liberty, ordered liberty, is to be a liberal of sorts, but not the kind who sees "no enemies to the Left," or who turns a blind eye to the totalitarian temptation with its cruel impulse to localize evil in suspects groups who are guilty less for what they have done than who they are. My qualified, if real and subordinate, liberalism is thus anti-totalitarian to the core.

I cherish civility and what Harvey C. Mansfield has called the "forms and formalities of liberty." But I disdain a faux moderation that succumbs, in whole or in part, to woke nostrums in a desperate effort to stay relevant or to have a seat at the progressivist table. True moderation should not be confused with a lukewarm acceptance—or rejection—of the old verities that still deserve our undying commitment, or a misbe-gotten belief that moderation is primarily "geographic," as if being in the middle in the struggle between good and evil, and truth and false-hood, is ever advisable. To succumb to the fantasies of gender ideology, for example, is to eschew reality and to reject human nature as in any way relevant to judging the thought and action of human beings. True moderation must always be grounded in the Real, in the natural order of things, if it is to be both efficacious and morally choice-worthy.

This author prays every day that the "center will hold," to borrow a phrase from W. B. Yeats. But with Pierre Manent, I acknowledge that a "fanaticism of the center" has taken hold of what the late Angelo Codevilla called the "ruling class." These increasingly unaccountable elites defer blindly to the tyranny of experts, thoughtlessly prefer fashionable cos-mopolitanism or globalism to humane national loyalty and prefer fad-dish relativism and moral experimentation to the old moral norms. In contrast, true moderation requires what the classics called "order in the soul," salutary self-control and self-limitation guided by right reason, and not the emancipation of the human will from all humanizing—and civilizing—restraints. Too many contemporary liberals and centrists have forgotten the crucial moral, cultural, and spiritual preconditions of our political order. They dispense with them with remarkable ease. But liberty without law, including the moral law, is unworthy of human beings and is ultimately not in accord with the order of things.

To the so-called New Right, I caution against the urge to latch on to something superficially new, vital, and exciting at the expense of jettisoning the classical and Christian wisdom of old. Impatience with traditional affirmations, a distrust of biblical morality, and facile ap-peals to masculinity in place of spiritually demanding manliness, in the end provide an alluring road to nowhere. To be sure, one can delight in Friedrich Nietzsche's fierce poetic eloquence about the "last man" devoid of high aims and noble purposes. Nietzsche rightly takes aim at sentimental humanitarianism and a cult of tenderness that ignores the severe and demanding virtues. Nietzsche's evocative and thrilling rhetoric undeniably puffs young men up, making them feel like members of a small spiritual aristocracy of the wise and the strong.

But, in truth, true political and spiritual wisdom sides neither with rank sentimentality or the kind of cruelty and hardness celebrated by Nietzsche. Against the humanitarian Left and the atheistic Right, I instead recommend the noble and elevated conception of "political freedom" put forward by Tocqueville in his foreword to *The Old Regime and the Revolution*. In a particularly beautiful passage, Tocqueville noted that political freedom rightly understood "takes men out of themselves to live in a common world, providing the wisdom for judging their virtues and their vices; only political freedom allows them to see themselves both as equals and as distinct."[1]

In the spirit of Tocqueville and the American Founders, we are in pressing need of a return to rational debate and discussion. But such debate and discussion require crucial preconditions which we have forgotten at our peril. As Eric Voegelin argued in his 1965 essay, "What is Political Reality" (from his book *Anamnesis*), common sense long flourished in the Anglo-American tradition, keeping alive a truncated (if somewhat inarticulate) version of the rich and varied accounts of ethics and practical reason to be found in Aristotle's *Ethics* and Cicero's *On Duties*. In doing so, it largely kept irresponsible and ideological politics at bay. But already by the time Voegelin was writing in the mid-1960s, this tradition was fraying. Adherents of common sense were losing self-confidence and intellectual self-assurance. Common sense was losing its roots in the *ratio*, right reason in the form of intellection of the true, the good, and the beautiful, and in the political realm, in some larger understanding of the virtue of *phronesis* or practical reason, and how to cultivate it. In his essay, Voegelin tellingly added that common sense, as precious as it is, cannot begin to overcome the ideological deformation of reality without a vigorous return to right reason (what the Greeks and Romans called *nous* and *ratio*) in all its amplitude. That return requires the renewal of liberal and civic education as humanizing enterprises fully committed to the pursuit of wisdom about the best way for human beings to live. Only then can the dignity of republican self-government be appreciated once again by citizens attuned to the good use of freedom and the rewards and challenges of lives well lived. The road forward is steep, but the resources for civilizational renewal are still available to all those who seek them.

TEN ESSENTIAL BOOKS
FOR UNDERSTANDING
AND OVERCOMING
THE IDEOLOGICAL LIE

EDMUND BURKE, *Reflections on the Revolution in France*. This classic of political philosophy is available in many editions, almost all of which are serviceable. I recommend the edition published in 2003 by Yale University Press in its "Rethinking the Western Tradition" series (with some helpful accompanying essays, particularly the one by Irish man of letters and Burke biographer Conor Cruise O'Brien). Burke was the first great statesman and political thinker to truly discern the evils of "armed doctrine," "atheism by establishment," as well as the despotism inherent in the spirit of (revolutionary) abstraction liberated from prudence, moderation, and salutary tradition. Burke was an anti-totalitarian avant la lettre. And his recommendation of a "manly, moral, and regulated liberty" remains as relevant as ever.

DOSTOEVSKY, *Demons*. Among the many translations of this indispensable work, I recommend the one by Richard Pevear and Larissa Volokhonsky published by Vintage Classics in 1994. Dostoevsky, the artist and novelist, remains the most discerning critic of revolutionary nihilism and revolutionary terrorism, of the hatred for creation that animates them from beginning to end. Better than anyone before or since, he captures the grotesque spiritual pathology that leads deracinated intellectuals to want to destroy the world as it is rather than to improve it in accord with spiritually elevating standards of truth and beauty.

SOLZHENITSYN, *The Gulag Archipelago*. This multifaceted "experiment in literary investigation" is also available in multiple editions. I recommend the 2018 paperback edition of the authorized abridgement published by Vintage Classics (with a foreword by Jordan B. Peterson) and the

2023 fiftieth anniversary commemorative hardcover edition published by Vintage Classics (with an introduction by Natalia Solzhenitsyn). *The Gulag Archipelago* provides a searing, artful, and truly incomparable indictment of Communist totalitarianism and all its works. At its deepest level, it takes aim at ideological Manichæism in all its forms and recovers the drama of good and evil at the heart of individual and collective life.

The Great Lie, edited and introduced by F. Flagg Taylor IV. Published in 2011 by ISI Books, this indispensable anthology collects the best "Classic and Recent Appraisals of Ideology and Totalitarianism," in the apt words of its subtitle. The anthologized authors include Alain Besançon, Martin Malia, Raymond Aron, Hannah Arendt, Aleksandr Solzhenitsyn, Eric Voegelin, Czesław Milosz, Claude Lefort, Leszek Kołakowski, and Václav Havel, among others. A book to be returned to again and again.

ERIC VOEGELIN, *Hitler and the Germans*. Based on lectures delivered at the University of Munich in 1964, this profound book, available in paperback from the University of Missouri Press, chronicles the descent of Germany into the ideological abyss of National Socialism. With remarkable lucidity and a proper degree of righteous anger, the Austrian-born political philosopher chronicles the intellectual and spiritual pathologies that gave rise to Hitlerism, as well as the shameful complicity of the churches, universities, and the legal establishment (in whole or part) in its rise. This book richly illustrates Voegelin's notion of ideology as "Second Reality," a "metaphysically mad" (as Burke famously put it) effort to replace human nature and the human condition with a "surreal," fictive, and deeply destructive alternative reality.

The Long Night of the Watchman: Essays by Václav Benda, 1977–1989, edited by F. Flagg Taylor IV and published by Saint Augustine Books in 2018. These deeply reflective essays by a Czech Catholic dissident writer brilliantly capture the effects of totalitarian mendacity on the human soul. But rejecting passivity and civic withdrawal, Benda traces the path for building a "parallel polis" to accompany the necessary rejection of the Ideological Lie. His ideas remain remarkably applicable today as we confront new forms of despotism in the Western world.

RYSZARD LEGUTKO, *The Demon in Democracy: Totalitarian Temptations in a Free Society.* Originally published by Encounter Books in 2016, this prescient book foresaw how corrupted forms of "liberal democracy" (already evident in post-Communist Europe in the years after 1989) mirrored Communism with its fanciful progressivism, dismissal of the wisdom of the past, and the jettisoning of the venerable standards of judgment provided by truth, beauty, and goodness. A jarring yet thoroughly enlightening book.

NIGEL BIGGAR, *Colonialism: A Moral Reckoning.* Written by a distinguished theologian and ethicist, this book, published by William Collins in 2023, provides an erudite, measured, and morally serious response to the frenzied indignation of postcolonial theory that increasingly dominates academic discussion and "discourse."

ROD DREHER, *Live Not by Lies: A Manual for Christian Dissidents.* In his lively, thoughtful, and inspiring 2020 book (published by Sentinel), Dreher renews Solzhenitsyn's great call to "live not by lies" in light of the rise of a post-Christian, pretotalitarian society in the Western world. Without hyperbole, he compellingly demonstrates that "it can happen here." But Dreher's book is ultimately a call to spiritual and political resistance, and not to mere withdrawal or despair.

JOSHUA MITCHELL, *American Awakening: Identity Politics and Other Afflictions of Our Time.* Mitchell's vitally important 2020 book (published by Encounter Books) provides both a deep spiritual meditation on the dislocations of the late-modern soul as well as a bracing clarion call to resist ideological Manichæism in its new racialist forms.

[139]

ENDNOTES

INTRODUCTION

1 *See* Aurel Kolnai, "Three Riders of the Apocalypse: Communism, Nazism, and Progressive Democracy" in Kolnai, *Privilege and Liberty and Other Essays in Political Philosophy*, ed. Daniel J. Mahoney (New York: Lexington Books, 1999), especially 105, 108, and 114–18.

2 Leo Strauss, "Progress or Return?" in *An Introduction to Political Philosophy: Ten Essays by Leo Strauss*, ed. Hilail Gildin (Detroit: Wayne State University, 1989), 264.

3 Aleksandr Solzhenitsyn, *The Gulag Archipelago: The Authorized Abridgement*, trans. Thomas P. Whitney and Harry Willetts (New York: Vintage, 2023), 75, 312.

4 Gerhart Niemeyer, *Between Nothingness and Paradise* (Indiana: St. Augustine's Press, 1998), 3, 41, 79, 94, 96–97, 102, 141–42, 201.

5 Niemeyer, *Nothingness*.

6 Roger Scruton, *An Intelligent Person's Guide to Modern Culture* (Indiana: Saint Augustine's Press, 2000), 126, 130, 132, 138, 145–46.

7 I have drawn freely from Mark Dooley's excellent discussion in *Roger Scruton: The Philosopher on Dover Beach: An Intellectual Biography* (New York: Bloomsbury, 2024), 165–67.

8 I am quoting from an exchange between Manent and Alain Finkielkraut on the wisdom of legalizing euthanasia ("La Grande Confrontation") that appeared in the French monthly *L'incorrect*, no. 72 (February 2024), 27–32. For the longer quotation, see 27–28.

9 *See* Dominique Schnapper, *The Democratic Spirit of Law* (New Jersey: Transaction Publishers, 2016), especially 15, 41, 177–80, and 177 for the longer quotation.

CHAPTER 1

1 All references to Christopher F. Rufo, *America's Cultural Revolution: How the Revolution Conquered Everything* (New York: Broadside Books, 2020) will be cited parenthetically as *ACR* followed by the relevant page numbers. Rufo's book surpasses any other existing account of the deep roots of wokeism in the mating of the New Left with what I call throughout this book the new racialism (which is as inherently racist as the old). I am indebted to his richly serious account and dissection of the woke Left.

2 "What Does Our Nation Mean to Us? Rejecting the Culture of Hate," Real Clear Politics, July 2, 2020.

3 *See* his July 4, 1852, speech "What to the Slave Is the Fourth of July?" Douglass's riveting address perfectly captures the wounded pride of black men who live in a republic that tolerated chattel slavery, as well as Douglass's own considered judgment that the U.S. Constitution was in decisive respects a "GLORIOUS LIBERTY DOCUMENT." Any decent anthology of Douglass's writings will include the address, including those available from Yale University Press and the Library of America.

4 *See* John O'Sullivan's foreword to Ryszard Legutko, *Demon in Democracy*, trans. Teresa Adelson (New York: Encounter Books, 2016), vi. O'Sullivan's is an illuminating account of traditional liberal democracy versus the more recent version of the regime of the same name that has capitulated to its "liberationist instincts."

5 *See*, for example, "The peace women," *The New Criterion*, vol. 42, no. 5 (January 2024).

6 "'How Elites Ate the Social Justice Movement' Review: Left Against Itself," *The Wall Street Journal*, August 26, 2023.

7 *See Neither Victims nor Executioners: An Ethic Superior to Murder*, trans. Dwight MacDonald (Oregon: Wipf & Stock, 2008). No pacifist, Camus is nonetheless groping for "an ethic superior to murder." Unlike Jean-Paul Sartre, he had the dignity and good sense to reject totalitarianism in both theory and practice. For Camus, there was no "necessary murder" that should be applauded by decent thinking men.

8 Aleksandr Solzhenitsyn, *The Gulag Archipelago: 50th Anniversary Edition* (New York: Vintage Classics, 2023), hereafter cited parenthetically as *GA* followed by the appropriate pages. The Russian writer's rejection of every effort to localize evil in suspect parties, races, groups, and classes rather than in the drama of good and evil in every human heart provides the leitmotif for this book.

9 *See* his 1978 essay "The Power of the Powerless."

10 The nonagenarian black social scientist Thomas Sowell was the great scourge of the new ideological racialism avant la lettre. His lucid common sense and his fidelity to where the facts lead provide a humane model for all truly non- or anti-ideological social science. In particular, see Sowell, *Discrimination and Disparities* (New York: Basic Books, 2019) and *Social Justice Fallacies* (New York: Basic Books, 2023).

11 Carson Holloway, *Up from Conservatism: Revitalizing the Right after a Generation of Decay*, ed. Arthur Milikh (New York: Encounter Books, 2023). Holloway's essay provides a compelling critique of a conservatism that reduces itself to little more than the defense of abstract propositional truths rather than of a self-governing republic (and nation) whose moral foundations are under assault.

12 *Democracy in America*, eds. and trans. Harvey Mansfield and Delba Winthrop (Chicago: University of Chicago Press, 2000) 411–16, hereafter cited parenthetically as *DIA* followed by the appropriate page reference.

13 *See* his 1796 "Two Letters Addressed to a Member of the Present Parliament on the Proposals for Peace with the Regicide Directory of France."

CHAPTER 2

1 "A Simple Way the Republican House Can Combat the Woke Left," *The Wall Street Journal*, January 13, 2023.

2 "Charles Dickens" in *Inside the Whale and Other Essays* (London: Victor Gollancz Ltd., 1940), 84.

3 *See*, for example, his April 21, 2022, address at the Stanford University Cyber Policy Symposium, entitled "Challenges to Democracy in the Digital Information Realm."

4 "The Seer of Prague," *New Republic*, vol. 205, no. 1 (July 1991), 35–40.

5 Paul Johnson, *Modern Times: The World from the Twenties to the Nineties, Revised Edition* (New York: Harper Collins, 1991), 506–43. Johnson's iconoclastic history of the twentieth century remains required reading for all thoughtful and inquiring partisans of Western civilization.

6 *See*, for example, "We All Live on Campus Now," *New York Magazine*, February 9, 2018.

7 *See* Robert Faurisson, *Mémoire en défense: contre ceux qui m'accusant de falsifier l'histoire* (Paris: La vielle taupe, 1980).

CHAPTER 3

1 *See* "The Letter to the Soviet Leaders" in Solzhenitsyn, *East and West* (New York: Harper Perennial, 1980), 120. Hereafter, *East and West* will be referred to in the text as *EW* followed by the appropriate page numbers.

2   *See* Solzhenitsyn, "Live Not By Lies!", trans. Yermolai Solzhenitsyn, in *The Solzhenitsyn Reader: New And Essential Writings, 1947–2005*, eds. Edward E. Ericson Jr. and Daniel J. Mahoney (Washington, DC: ISI Books, 2006), hereafter cited as *TSR* followed by the pertinent page number. *The Solzhenitsyn Reader* provides ready access to all of Solzhenitsyn's major texts.

3   *See*, for example, *How to Be a Conservative* (New York: Bloomsbury, 2015).

4   *See* Weiss, "We Got Here Because of Cowardice. We Get Out With Courage," *Commentary*, November, 2021.

5   Václav Benda's provocative and newly relevant essays on the "parallel polis" can be found in *The Long Night of the Watchman: Essays by Václav Benda, 1977–1989*, ed. F. Flagg Taylor IV (South Bend: St. Augustine's Press, 2017), 49–56, 211–21.

6   On this promising development to recover thoughtful and sympathetic teaching and scholarship about the American civic tradition, see Jenna Storey, "Follow the Left's Example to Reform Higher Ed," in *The Wall Street Journal*, January 27, 2024.

CHAPTER 4

1   *See* P. T. Bauer, *Equality, the Third World and Economic Delusion* (Cambridge: Harvard University Press, 1981), hereafter cited parenthetically in the body of the text as *ETWED* followed by the appropriate page number.

2   Thomas Sowell, *Conquests and Cultures: An International History* (New York: Basic Books, 1995), hereafter cited parenthetically in the body of the text as *CC*, followed by the appropriate page number.

3   Girard, *I See Satan Fall Like Lightning* (New York: Orbis Books, 2001), 179.

4   Hereafter cited parenthetically as *CAMR*, followed by the appropriate page number.

5   Nasrin Pourhamrang, "'Things Fall Apart' Now More Famous Than Me, Says Chinua Achebe, *Daily Trust*, September 8, 2012.

6   *See* Tocqueville, "Testimony Against Slavery."

7   Quoted in Gary Scott Smith, *Duty and Destiny: The Life and Faith of Winston Churchill* (Grand Rapids: William B. Eerdmans, 2021), 153.

8   *See* "The Clemency of the Conqueror" (1919) in Churchill, *The Power of Words: His Remarkable Life Recounted Through His Writings and Speeches*, ed. Martin Gilbert (New York: Hachette Books, 2012), 154–155.

CHAPTER 5

1   *See* Marcel Gauchet, *Robespierre: The Man Who Divides Us the Most* (Princeton: Princeton University Press, 2022), henceforth cited in the body of the text parenthetically as *R* followed by the appropriate page number.

2   I have drawn on *Robespierre: Virtue and Terror*, presented and introduced by Slavoj Žižek (New York: Verso Books, 2007), henceforth cited parenthetically as *RVT* followed by the relevant page number.

3   Scruton, *Fools* (London: Bloomsbury, 2019), 84.

CHAPTER 6

1   *See The Marx-Engels Reader*, ed. Robert C. Tucker (New York: W. W. Norton & Company, 1978), hereafter cited parenthetically as *MER* followed by the appropriate page numbers.

2   Leszek Kołakowski, "The Marxist Roots of Stalinism" (1977), *The Great Lie: Classic and Recent Reappraisals of Ideology and Totalitarianism*, ed. F. Flagg Taylor IV (Washington, DC: ISI Books, 2011), 156–76.

3   Raymond Aron, *Memoirs: Fifty Years of Political Reflection*, trans. George Holoch (New Jersey: Holmes & Meier, 1990), 468–69, hereafter cited parenthetically as *M* followed by the relevant pages.

4   In addition to the writings of Marx himself, the reader could profitably benefit from an engagement with the venomous prose and totalitarian machinations of V. I. Lenin, the founder of the Soviet revolutionary state itself. See *The Lenin Anthology*, ed. Robert C. Tucker (New York: W. W. Norton & Company, 1975). These writings provide a warning against a mode of thinking and discourse that needs to be scrupulously avoided, the "total critique" of society of which Gerhart Niemeyer has spoken.

5   (South Bend: Gateway Publishing, 1968), 27–28.

6   *See* Manent, *Modern Liberty and Its Discontents*, eds. Daniel J. Mahoney and Paul Seaton (New York: Rowman & Littlefield, 1998), 119.

CHAPTER 7

1   (New York: Vintage, 1994), cited hereafter parenthetically as *D* followed by the appropriate page number.

2   Both "The Peasant Marei" and "Pushkin Speech" can be found in *A Dostevskii Companion: Texts and Contexts*, eds. Katherine Bowers, Connor Doak, and Kate Holland (Boston: Academic Studies Press, 2018), hereafter cited in parentheses as *DC* followed by the appropriate pages.

CHAPTER 8

1   Francis Fukuyama, "The End of History?" *National Interest*, no. 16 (Summer 1989).

2   Raymond Aron, *In Defense of Decadent Europe* (New Jersey: Transaction Publishers, 1996).

3   *See* John Paul II, "Address of John Paul II at Czestochowa, Jasna Górna," June 4, 1997, which is available readily online.

4   (New York: Alfred A. Knopf), 5.

5   "A World Split Apart" in *The Solzhenitsyn Reader*.

6   The remarkable comparison between decayed liberal democracy and Communist totalitarianism can be found in Ryszard Legutko, *The Demon in Democracy: Totalitarian Temptations in a Free Society* (New York: Encounter Books, 2018), 138–39. Legutko's book is both prescient and discerning, and thus bound to be controversial.

7   *See* Caldwell, "Hungary and the Future of Europe," *Claremont Review of Books*, vol. 19, no. 2 (Spring 2019).

8   This luminous passage can be found in the chapter "The Ascent" from the abridged version of *The Gulag Archipelago*, with a foreword by Jordan Peterson (London: Vintage, 2018), 312. Peterson's lucid and penetrating foreword, an eloquent and forceful warning against ideological Manichæism in all its forms, is highly recommended. Peterson makes clear that the ideological virus is taking on new and dangerously virulent forms throughout the Western world. History, most assuredly, has not come to an end.

CHAPTER 9

1   *See The 1619 Project: A New Origin Story*, eds. Nikole Hannah-Jones, Caitlin Roper, Ilena Silverman, and Jake Silverstein (New York: One World, 2021), cited parenthetically hereafter as *1619* followed by the appropriate page reference.

2   Mary Grabar, *Debunking the 1619 Project: Exposing the Plan to Divide America* (Washington, DC: Regnery, 2021), cited parenthetically hereafter as *Debunking* followed by the appropriate page numbers.

3 *See* Peter W. Wood, *1620: A Critical Response to the 1619 Project* (New York: Encounter Books, 2020), hereafter cited parenthetically as *1620* followed by the appropriate page reference.

4 (New York: Encounter Books), hereafter cited parenthetically hereafter as *AA* followed by the appropriate page numbers.

CHAPTER 10

1 For a thoughtful journalistic account of the underlying affinities between relativism, subjectivism, and fanaticism, see Karlo Broussard, *The New Relativism: Unmasking the Philosophy of Today's Woke Moralists* (California: Catholic Answers Press, 2023).

2 Michael Polanyi, *The Logic of Liberty* (Indiana: Liberty Fund, 1998), hereafter cited parenthetically as *LL* followed by the appropriate page reference.

3 Scruton, *Modern Culture*, 126.

4 Scruton, *Modern Culture*, 135–148.

CHAPTER 11

1 Bertrand de Jouvenel, *Sovereignty: An Inquiry into the Political Good* (Indianapolis: Liberty Fund, 1997), 317.

2 Daniel J. Mahoney, *The Statesman as Thinker: Portraits of Greatness, Courage, and Moderation* (New York: Encounter Books, 2022).

3 Charles de Gaulle, *The Enemy's House Divided*, trans. Robert Eden (Raleigh: University of North Carolina Press, 2002), 1–3.

4 Scruton, *Modern Culture*, 131.

CONCLUSION

1 Alexis de Tocqueville, *The Ancien Régime and the Revolution*, ed. Jon Elster, trans. Arthur Goldhammer (New York: Cambridge University Press, 2011), 17.

INDEX

Roberts, Dorothy, 109
Robespierre, Maximilien, 59–67; Cassat the Elder, ultimate paradox quoted by, 65; "disposition to impersonality," 61; French monarchy, Burke's statement about, 63; hatred of Christianity, 64; marred "liberalism" of, 62; new Jacobins, 66; revolutionary principles defended by, 62; "Rights of Man," 59, 60; sources and suggested readings, 67; "wisdom of Montesquieu," 60
Robespierre: The Man Who Divides Us the Most (Gauchet), 59
Roosevelt, Franklin D., 15
Roosevelt, Teddy, 11
Rousseau, 61, 71
Rufo, Christopher, 11, 12, 13, 15, 124

Schnapper, Dominique, 7–8
Science, Politics, and Gnosticism (Voegelin), 74
Screech, Matthew, 88
Scruton, Roger, 5, 7, 36, 66, 67, 72, 124, 125, 131
Second Reality, 1, 5, 17, 44, 129
Serra, Saint Junípero, 11
1776 Unites, 175
Shakespeare, William, 26
Singh, Manmohan, 57
1619 Project, 13, 45, 103–17; assault on America by, 106; book of essays on, 105–6; books debunking, 108, 111; criticism of, 104, 106; explanation of naming, 103; as expression of Ideological Lie, 103; first appearance of, 104; irresponsible rhetorical trope of, 111; lazy polemic of, 107; patriotism ignored by contributors to the project, 105; recharacterization of Lincoln by, 107; slavery and, 103, 109–10; sources and suggested readings, 116–17; wokeness and, 112–16
1619 Project: A New Origin Story, The, 106
1620: A Critical Response to the 1619 Project (Wood), 111
slavery: Burke's despising of, 55; historical ubiquity of, 111; Lincoln's opposition to, 109
Social Contract (Rousseau), 61
"social-justice warriors," 15
social-media companies, woke personnel within, 22
Solzhenitsyn, Aleksandr, 7, 17, 28, 41, 67, 101, 137 38; diagnosis of Marx by, 74; on Dostoevsky's foreseeing of totalitarianism, 77; dramatic proposal to compatriots, 34, 38; foundations of Communist regimes noted by, 31; Ideological Lie experienced by, 31, 32–33; Ideological Lie termed by, 123; remark about Dostoevsky, 77
Solzhenitsyn, Natalia, 138
Solzhenitsyn Reader: New and Essential Writings, The (Mahoney and Ericson, eds.), 87
Soros, George, 99
Sovereignty: An Inquiry into the Political Good (Jouvenel), 127
Soviet Communism, 71, 89.
    See also Communism